A Journey through Advent

A spiritual focus for personal or group use

A 31-DAY GUIDE

REV DR ROB FROST

Contents

Introduction   5

How to Use *A Journey through Advent*   7

WEEK ONE
Isaiah's Journey   9

WEEK TWO
John's Journey   27

WEEK THREE
Mary's Journey   49

WEEK FOUR
Jesus' Journey   67

WEEK FIVE
Our Journey   83

Introduction

A devotional journey through the season of Advent

A few months ago I walked the 'three peaks', Ben Nevis, Scafell and Snowdon. It was a demanding but exhilarating experience, and a journey I will never forget. About eighty people joined me on this journey, and it was a great opportunity to pray and seek God as well as to walk through some of the most spectacular scenery in the UK.

There were times when the path ahead seemed impossible to climb, and times when we were totally exhausted. There were times of great jubilation as we scaled the highest peak and times of real darkness as the clouds gathered and the rain fell. At the outset, however, we had decided that we would make the journey, whatever the personal cost. It was grim determination which kept some of us going when we really felt like giving up!

This devotional journey through the season of Advent follows the journeys of some of the key characters in the Advent season. As we walk alongside them, my prayer is that you will be strengthened and encouraged in the journey that you are called to make. You will sense their struggles, and get to understand some of their battles.

If you are going to make this Advent journey this year, it will take a similar kind of determination and commitment. Many things will crowd in to distract you, many pressures will tempt you to 'give up'! Yet, if you do manage to make this month-long journey I sincerely believe that you'll find it very worthwhile, and that, spiritually, you'll feel fitter and healthier at the end than when you set out!

This devotional journey is especially designed for people who have been struggling with their devotional life. Maybe you've felt just too busy to pray or read the Bible recently. Maybe you've been through a particularly tough time, and haven't felt like getting close to God. Or maybe you've never really got started on the devotional life at all.

If that's you, then this is a journey you really need to make. This guidebook is designed to help you to take the first steps, like a toddler just beginning to walk. It's written to support you, like a physio helping someone to walk after a long and debilitating illness. It's devised to show you the way, like a mountain guide who knows the path because of his years of experience.

The season of Advent can be one of the busiest times of the year. In the run-up to Christmas the pace of activity at work, college and school can become unbearable.

Here then is the road map to a devotional journey that you can build into your lifestyle in those hectic weeks before and after Christmas.

How to use *A Journey through Advent*

Advent is growing in importance as a Christian festival, and it provides an ideal opportunity to explore some of the richest aspects of our Christian faith. Many Christians are setting aside the weeks before Christmas as a particular focus for their devotional and prayer life. *A Journey through Advent* is designed to help Christians to make their own journey alone, or with the support and encouragement of a group.

For Personal Use
The material is designed to be used for the 31 days of the month of December and requires a commitment of about fifteen minutes per day.

For Use in a Group
This is 'easy to use' material, and could almost be used 'self-help' style by the group members. It does not require a lot of preparation by a leader!

The material can be used for five sessions in an existing housegroup or a special Advent group. To get the most out of the material each of the group should make a commitment to use the personal devotional material each day.

The section headed 'Reflect or discuss' each day can be used to think through issues yourself, for devotions together with one or two others, or for use in an Advent study group at the end of the week.

The group material is found at the end of each week's notes. So the group members need to start using the book one week before the first session! A typical group might receive and start using the study guide by 17 November, and meet on 24 November, 1, 8 and 15 December. There is optional material in the last three daily sections which could be used for a fifth group meeting after Christmas or as the first session for a new year housegroup series (eg on 5 January).

Leader's note

There are three resources for each group meeting.

1) Questions based on each day's reading which should stimulate discussion (the 'Reflect or discuss' sections at the end of each day). Some groups may simply like to re-visit the seven days of material, and ask a different group member to lead the discussion based on one of the days.

2) A devotional meditation is provided for each group meeting. This could be used with a CD of Christmas music and accompanied by the lighting of Advent candles. There are other prayers and poems scattered throughout the book which could also be used here.

3) The 'Coffee and Chat' material points to a social or political issue highlighted by the material. Some groups might like to read it and focus on the issue highlighted for the final part of the evening while coffee is served! This is provided to answer the criticism that sometimes study group material is so 'heavenly minded' that it doesn't relate to important everyday issues.

Rob Frost
December 2003

Isaiah's Journey

1 DEC

A certain future in an uncertain age!

Our journey begins with Isaiah as he discovers that beyond the uncertainties of today there are things of which we can be certain tomorrow.

Advent is a season for thinking about the future. It's a time for placing all our insecurities into the context of God's perfect plan and eternal purposes.

The Word

Isaiah was facing a very uncertain future. The neighbouring country, Assyria, was on the march. Their aggressive king Tiglath-Pileser the third was looking towards Israel to expand his territory. His troops arrived in the northern part of Israel, and started to deport whole communities to his territory deep within Assyria.

Imagine, if you were Isaiah, what that would feel like! All your future plans are now put on hold. Your hopes for your nation lie in ruins. Friends and family are disappearing to a place where you'll never see them again. And all the time the threat of violence is getting closer to you and the ones you love.

But God spoke to Isaiah in this dark and frightening experience – and Isaiah prophesied what he heard.

Read Isaiah 2:1–5.

In this wonderful vision, Isaiah sees beyond the armies of Assyria, beyond the deportation of his people, beyond a dark and uncertain time, to a day when God's house is established in the highest place of all. The Lord will sort out this aggressive and violent nationalistic enemy, weapons will be melted down and their metal used for more peaceful purposes!

Pause for thought

It is this certainty of God's ultimate victory that has kept Christians going through the darkest days of oppression and persecution. We rejoice that God will ultimately have 'the last word' of history and that one day He will set all wrongs right.

On this first step of your Advent journey, consider your future.

> Make a list of all the things which make you feel afraid, uncertain or worried about the future. What frightens you or disturbs you most?

Punch line

Advent is about looking to the future – not with fear and uncertainty – but with optimism and confidence.

On this first day of our Advent journey, let's get things straight! The end of the story is that God wins and that one day we will see Jesus as the victorious King! The great blessing of being an Advent Christian is that we live in that victory now! The future is no longer a mystery, because we've read the last page, and we know that we made the right choices!

A time to pray

Dear Lord Jesus,
I bring before You all my uncertainties and all my fears.
Please don't let these things dominate my life,
or cast shadows over my days.
Don't let fear of tomorrow tinge today's moments with darkness.
Rather, may all my tomorrows safely lead
to the awesome mountain of Your love:
A place of shelter
A place of security
A place of Eternal rest in You.

Pray for others
- Pray for those who face an uncertain future:
  Because of war or because of famine ...
  or because of ill health or brokenness.
  (Name people in your own family, church or community who
  need strength to face an uncertain future.)
    It's interesting to note that the words of Isaiah 2:4 are carved in
  stone outside the United Nations building in New York. They are
  words which should bring confidence and courage to all who
  work toward peace in the world. Words which should keep us
  all going – even when the going gets tough.
- Pray for those who are the peacemakers of the world.

Reflect or discuss
- Try to imagine what it must have been like to have lived where
  Isaiah lived. What were the people thinking about, talking about,
  worrying about?
- In that context what must Isaiah's prophecy have given them?
- 'Come, let us go up to the mountain of the LORD, to the house of
  the God of Jacob. He will teach us his ways ...' (Isa. 2:3). Imagine
  yourself approaching the Holy Place, God's everlasting throne, on
  the mountain. What would it feel like, sound like, look like?
- What frightens you or disturbs you most about the future? Is it ill-
  health or unemployment, the breakdown of a relationship or the
  possibility of a terrorist attack?
    Place your fears, your uncertainties and your insecurities at the
  feet of a God who knows you, understands you and loves you.
  Place whatever you're facing in the context of His ultimate victory.
- Read again Isaiah 2:1–5, and turn the words into your own prayers
  of faith and hope for all your tomorrows.

2 DEC

Bright light in dark days

Our journey with Isaiah continues as he discovers that beyond the darkness of his current situation God's light will one day shine. Advent is a season for candles and lights. Today gives us an opportunity to focus on the Light of Christ.

The Word

Isaiah was certainly passing through a very dark time. He despaired of Ahaz, the king of Judah. Ahaz had raided the holy Temple and stolen from the treasury in order to appease Tiglath-Pileser the third, the Assyrian king. Even worse, Ahaz had been dazzled by the glitz of a pagan shrine in Assyria, and, in another attempt to appease the Assyrian king, had installed the same kind of pagan shrine in the Temple itself.

It's hard for us to understand what this act of sacrilege must have meant to God-fearing Israelites like Isaiah. The sacred space had been corrupted. The very doors of the Temple had been flung open and the forces of evil had poured in. The purity of God's house had been compromised. These were very dark days for Isaiah and for all God's people.

It was into this darkness that Isaiah spoke a very powerful prophecy. It was a poignant message for Ahaz and the people of Isaiah's generation, but it also speaks to us today. His message was delivered in a tense which scholars call 'the prophetic perfect'. It's used to describe an event which, though yet to happen, is spoken of as if it has already come to pass. That's real faith!

Many Christians believe that, as Isaiah spoke this prophecy to the people of his generation, he was also reaching towards God's ultimate purpose in sending Jesus as the light of the world to help us even in our days of deepest darkness.

Read Isaiah 9:2–7.

This prophecy glimpses a picture of Jesus – not just the Jesus of Bethlehem, but the Jesus who is glorified and worshipped. The Jesus described in Revelation who reigns for ever and ever!

Pause for thought

One of the greatest joys of being a Christian is that we have a friend who is a 'Wonderful Counsellor'. His understanding of us and of our situation is perfect and complete. He has promised that, even in the darkest of days, He will never leave us or forsake us. In these early days of Advent we celebrate those who saw His coming from ancient times, and we celebrate His coming to us today.

On this second step of our Advent journey we think about dark days that we've faced.

It's easy to lose faith and to be drained of hope. Sometimes we can feel as though even God has deserted us! Maybe, even now, God seems far away from you and you're struggling to experience the presence of the Lord in your everyday life.

> **Read again Isaiah 9:2-7, and bathe in the light of the Presence of Jesus Christ.**

Punch line

Advent is about discovering the One whom Isaiah described as 'the great light'. We ask Him to flood us and fill us with the light of His presence. A light which the darkness can never extinguish. However deep our darkness may feel we should remember that, 'Of the increase of his government and of peace there will be no end'.

A time to pray

Jesus You are my
Wonderful Counsellor,
always ready to listen.
Jesus, You are my Mighty God,
supreme and majestic,
powerful and all-knowing.
Jesus, you are my
Everlasting Father,
Your love is wider than the ocean
and higher than the sky.
Jesus, You are my
Prince of Peace,
Your grace fills my life
Your love enfolds me each day.

Pray for others
- For those who face dark days spiritually …
- For those who have lost their faith in Jesus.

Reflect or discuss
- Read together: Isaiah 7:10–16
- How must Isaiah have felt about those days of darkness in the Temple?
- What do dark times feel like?
- What's the brightest light you've ever seen?
- If we really believed this prophecy how would it shape our relationship with Jesus?

---

3 DEC

Towards a new world

Our third day of following in Isaiah's footsteps gives us a glimpse of the kind of suffering he knew and of the glorious hope that sustained him through it. Advent is a season for looking at the world through different eyes! Historians look at the world of today and see the past, pundits look at the world of today and see the fashionable and transient. Advent Christians, however, look at the world and see God's perfect future fast approaching.

The Word
Isaiah was living in a place where there was much suffering. The Assyrians had staged a three-year siege over the whole region of Samaria. We can only imagine what kind of suffering had been inflicted on the people there as they hung on month upon month in the vain hope of rescue. When the fighting was over, the battle lost and the siege ended, huge numbers of Samaritan people were deported from Israel into Assyria. They became the 'disappeared'. It was an early example of the erosion of human rights and it had all the hallmarks of the 'ethnic cleansing' which we have seen in recent history.

Isaiah spoke prophetic words of comfort and hope into this bitter and painful situation. Words which not only applied to his generation but which reached forward to the coming of Jesus. Words which will be fulfilled when Jesus Christ returns and when He rights all wrongs.

Read Isaiah 11:1–10.

Isaiah looks to a time when the awful suffering of his people will be over. In this coming era the lion will lie down with the lamb, the leopard with the kid, and the calf and the lion be led by a child.

Isaiah sees that one day God will send a leader like no other. He will be very different from the kings of Isaiah's day who were so willing to compromise the core values of their faith.

Pause for thought

Christians should be full of hope and optimism about the future. We don't see a world that is wearing down and wearing out, but we look to a new world where all things will be redeemed, and where suffering will be no more.

Anyone who has walked the long corridors of a hospital at night will have seen the glimmer of individual bed-lights. The long dark hours of the night can seem to last for ever if you are facing overwhelming pain, fear or uncertainty.

On this third day of our Advent journey we think about different kinds of suffering. We can suffer emotionally, physically, even spiritually.

- Looking back across the years of your life, try to picture a time when you experienced suffering or when you walked that difficult path with someone you care about. Maybe you are travelling through the wilderness of suffering today; if so, how does it feel?
- Read again Isaiah 11:1–10, and taste the new life that awaits you in Christ!

Punch line

Many non-believers see nothing beyond suffering but oblivion and extinction, but Christians should have an Advent perspective that is infused with real hope. This vision of God's perfect justice and eternal righteousness is what has kept Christians going through the fires of persecution and torture.

We know that we are heading for a new heaven and a new earth where 'he will wipe every tear from their eyes, and death will be no more'. It's a place where nothing in all creation can separate us from the love of God.

Christians were never promised a life free from suffering but we do view it differently. It's this confidence which keeps us going, even when our journey takes us through really traumatic experiences.

A time to pray

Lord, when I suffer,
give me Isaiah's vision
of a tomorrow
burnished with justice,
bright with hope,
brilliant with reconciliation.
A time when the earth shall be full of the knowledge
of the Lord,
as the waters cover the sea.

Pray for others

● Remember those who suffer …
   Emotionally
   Physically
   Spiritually
● Remember those who suffer
   Because of oppressive political regimes
   Because of wrongful imprisonment or deportation

Reflect or discuss

● Read Isaiah 11:1–10 and list the qualities of the King of the New World. How many are there?
● Have you ever gone through a time of suffering? What's it like?
● Picture a world as described in verses 6–9. What else do you think would be unusual in a world like this? How would it feel to live

in such a world?
- Do we just wait around for this new world to come, or are we supposed to prepare for it? If so … how?

4 DEC

Flowers in the desert

Today we accompany Isaiah through his painful experience of loss. His journey was traumatic – and he lost many of the things that were most important to him. Yet he was able to see beyond his own time. Advent is when we remember that we not only live in a world of loss, but we also inhabit a world that is yet to come. We see the desert like everyone else, but we also see the flowers that will one day bloom there!

The Word
By the year 722 BC, Israel had ceased to be a nation. The people of Israel had lost everything that had once made them proud. God's chosen people were now a broken, dispersed and shamed remnant. They had lost everything that had once made them great. Isaiah was speaking into a crippling loss of pride.

The people of Israel were facing a sense of deep national loss. The nation of Israel had rebelled against God, had compromised and were now facing God's judgment. Isaiah was speaking into a loss of innocence.

Following the ending of the Samaritan siege the area became a resettlement zone for thousands of displaced people from around the Assyrian empire. These refugees brought with them pagan beliefs and practices which corrupted the faith of the remaining population. Samaria became home to paganism and evil practices. Isaiah was speaking into a loss of faith.

Hundreds of years later, in the time of Jesus, the Samaritans were still despised by many Jews because they had compromised their faith in Isaiah's day. When Jesus made the Good Samaritan a hero and when He spoke to the woman of Samaria He was breaking all the taboos of His day!

Read Isaiah 35:1–10.

Isaiah's Advent vision looks toward a time when something will come which will be even greater than that which has been lost. It will be a time when the wilderness will blossom, when streams will flow freely through the desert – and when the 'ransomed of the LORD will return [and] enter Zion with singing'.

Pause for thought

Loss is a basic human experience. It can be traumatic, bitter and painful. Perhaps the most common example is bereavement, and the painful stages of grief which follow in its wake. But there are other experiences of loss, too. The loss of a special relationship, the loss of a job or the loss of a church fellowship, can trigger a sense of despair which can dominate our lives for months or even years.

> **Read again Isaiah 35:1–10. Smell the flowers in the desert and hear the sound of singing as you enter Zion!**

Punch line

As we face our own experiences of loss, we need to recognise that experience is not the end of the story. Our Advent hope is fulfilled when Jesus returns to redeem all things and to put all things right. It is this ultimate faith in God's redemptive purposes which keeps us travelling on a journey which is often punctuated by loss.

A time to pray

Lord Jesus Christ,
You are the Redeemer.
You take our experiences of loss
and make them bearable.
You take our pain of losing
and give us a vision of final reunion.
Energise our limp hands,
strengthen our rubbery knees,
for God is coming soon!
On His way to put things right

and redress all wrongs,
He's on His way!
To save us!

Pray for others
Remember those who live in times of great personal loss ...

Reflect or discuss
● Imagine how the people of Israel must have felt in their time
of loss.
● Have you ever experienced some kind of loss in your own life?
What was it like?
● What or who helped you to get through it?
● Do you ever feel like 'giving up'?
● What should 'keep us going' on life's journey?

5 DEC

The Word of God stands forever!

Isaiah's journey took him through an era of great evil and occult
practice. Those who stand firm against the flood of evil will one day
be rewarded for their faithfulness.

Advent reminds us that we can trust the Word of God which stands
for ever.

The Word
Isaiah was living in a spiritually dark place among people involved
with the occult and black magic. The Samaritans and the Assyrians
had built fertility shrines at every crossroads which became centres
of sexual debauchery.

People began to worship gods made of wood or clay, and they
offered sacrifices to statues of bull calves and phallic symbols.
Worshippers performed immoral acts for the goddess Asherah; they
worshipped cosmic forces, sky gods and goddesses, and frequented
the evil shrines of Baal. Some offered their sons and daughters as
burnt offerings and others indulged in magic, sorcery and the black

arts. It's little wonder that the judgment of God was on them.

The 'spiritual climate' in Isaiah's time, then, was at an all time low. The people had violated God's law. It could not have been easy to live for God or to speak for God in such an evil atmosphere.

Read: Isaiah 40:1–11.

In this powerful Advent prophecy, Isaiah saw a time in which the glory of God would be revealed. The power and might of human forces would wither like grass and fade like a dying flower. Evil practices would be swept away but the Word of our God would stand for ever.

Pause for thought

Isaiah's prophecy is a powerful encouragement to stand firm against New Age practices and occult activities in our own generation. These spiritual activities which seem so popular and successful today will fade with the rising sun.

Those who have taken the work of evangelism into the devil's territory can tell of the battles they have experienced. Those who live lives of purity and holiness can speak of the wily tactics of the 'enemy'. Those who seek to engage in spiritual warfare often testify to a real struggle with evil. We need to remember that – in all these situations – God's awesome power (v.10) but intimate gentleness (v.11), surround us.

> Read again Isaiah 40:1–11

Punch line

The cartoon image of a glaring devil with horns and a three-pronged pitchfork makes a mockery of one whose power is real and whose intentions are destructive. Even now his power is worthless because of Christ's victory on Calvary, but Advent reminds us that one day God's sovereign power will destroy evil completely!

A time to pray

Almighty God, give us grace, that we may cast away the works of darkness, and put upon us the armour of light, now in the time of this mortal life, in which Thy Son Jesus Christ came to visit us in great humility; that in the last day when he shall come again in his glorious majesty to judge both the quick and the dead, we may rise to the life immortal, through him who liveth and reigneth with Thee and the Holy Ghost now and ever. Amen.

(From the *Prayer Book*, first published 1549.)

Pray for others
For those who are beaten down by temptation and evil.

Reflect or discuss
● What do you think it must have been like to live through such evil days?
● There is a lot of beautiful imagery in this prophecy. Isaiah sees deserts, fields and flocks. Picture the different images and talk about the full richness of meaning that you find in each one of them.
● How does Isaiah's prophecy help us to deal with the power of evil today?
● What does it feel like to be oppressed by the evil one?

6 DEC

A new kind of leader!

Isaiah was disillusioned with the leaders of his day – but he saw that one day a new kind of leader would arrive. Advent is the season when we look to the One who came, who comes and who will come again. The leader of all – the Servant King!

The Word
Isaiah was very disillusioned with the political leaders of his day. In 735 BC King Ahaz became king of Judah, but he soon lapsed into paganism and did deals with the ruthless king of Assyria. Hoshea gained the throne of Israel by assassinating his predecessor, but he failed to stop Israel's desperate slide into paganism and presided

over the end of Israel as a nation.

Hezekiah took over as king of Judah in 729 BC. He was at first committed to cleaning up his country from its pagan influences. Soon, however, it appears he did a deal with some envoys from Babylon which led to the downfall of Jerusalem.

Isaiah's Servant Songs looked towards the coming of a very different kind of leader.

In the first 'Servant Song' we see that the coming Messiah will have the 'Spirit of God' and will bring justice to the nations.

Read: Isaiah 42:1–4.

In the second 'Servant Song' we see that the Servant is Messianic, and that He will come to restore the people of God. He will be a 'light for the Gentiles' and through Him salvation will be brought to the ends of the earth. This prophecy was quoted by Simeon in the Temple and we can read it again in Luke 2:32.

Read: Isaiah 49:1–7.

Pause for thought

Sometimes we can get very disillusioned by the broken promises, false hopes or duplicitous lifestyles of our leaders. In the murky world of politics it's sometimes hard to know whom we can trust.

In these two 'Servant Songs' Isaiah looks to the day when God will send a different kind of leader: someone who can be trusted, looked up to and through whom God will achieve all His purposes.

- **What were the faithful people in Israel looking for, hoping for, waiting for?**
- **Think about the way in which Jesus fulfilled their hopes and dreams.**

Punch line

All through history God's prophets have looked forward to a different kind of leader. Not a King, but a servant. Not wrapped in finery, but broken and wounded. Not resting on the popularity of the crowd, but despised and rejected. Someone filled with God. This Leader can be our Leader too!

A time to pray
Think about the life of Jesus and thank God that He sent a different kind of leader!

Pray for others
Pray for those who have winter, but no Christmas, and who do not know the leadership of Jesus in their lives …

Reflect and respond
● Which of the Gospel stories about Jesus illustrate the way that He came as a Servant King?
● Turn these two 'Servant Songs' into prayers of thanksgiving for the One whom God has sent to us.
● Why do you think Jesus came as a Servant?
● What does this say to us about 'greatness' in God's kingdom?

7 DEC
___

The Saviour of the world

The wonderful news of Advent is that the coming Messiah will be a Saviour. Today we pause to remember just what that means!

The Word
As we conclude our journey with Isaiah we reach two of his most beautiful and poignant prophecies. They are frequently read at Advent services and Christmas carol concerts. Isaiah's vision of the Messiah was given over 700 years before Jesus came, and it gives us a rich insight into the unfolding purposes of God.

Read: Isaiah 52:7–10.

The final 'Servant Song' is often seen as the most important Old Testament passage about Jesus. He is depicted as a despised and disfigured servant who bore the suffering and pain of others. He was pierced for the sins of others and His wounds brought healing.

Read: Isaiah 52:13–53:12.

Pause for thought

We have walked with Isaiah through his dark and difficult days. Yet he constantly looked beyond the misery of his everyday life to the fulfilment of God's purposes. He saw a bright hope-packed tomorrow and it gave him the strength to face the stress of each new day.

Isaiah knew that God is working His purposes out and that, ultimately, He will prevail! Isaiah's message was focused on God's ultimate victory. He looked towards the arrival of a new kind of leader who would save the people.

Punch line

Advent faith finds its fulfilment in the coming of the Lord Jesus Christ, whose suffering and death bring redemption, hope and salvation to all who put their trust in Him.

Talkabout

If you are in a group, you could use the 'Reflect or discuss' sections from the last six days as a basis for discussion.

Meditation

At the close of our Advent journey with Isaiah we pause to meditate.

You may like to light an Advent candle in a darkened room, play some Christmas music on the stereo, and read our first Advent meditation by candlelight! You can do this alone – or as part of an Advent group.

Pause to think about what you have learnt and felt during the last six days of these studies.

We're going to use the *Corde Natus*, one of the great Latin hymns, as our theme for meditation. This hymn is thought to have originated from the writings of Prudentius Aurelius Clemens who lived from about AD 348 to 410. He was a devout and cultured Spaniard who wrote poetry, was a lawyer and entered a monastery in middle age.

This nineteenth-century translation is by J.M. Neale, and sums up much of what we have been studying in Isaiah this week.

Of the Father's love begotten,
Ere the world began to be,
He is Alpha and Omega,
He the source, the ending he,
Of the things that are, that have been,
And that future years shall see,
Evermore and evermore.

This is he whom seers i' old time
Chanted of with one accord,
Whom the voices of the prophets
Promised in their faithful word;
Now he shines, the long expected;
Let creation praise its Lord,
Evermore and evermore.

O ye heights of heaven, adore him;
Angel hosts, let praises sing;
All dominions, bow before him.
And extol our God and King;
Let no tongue on earth be silent,
Every voice in concert ring,
Evermore and evermore.

Christ, to thee, with God the Father,
And O Holy Ghost, to thee,
Hymn and chant, and high thanksgiving,
And unwearied praises be,
Honour, glory, and dominion,
And eternal victory,
Evermore and evermore.

Coffee and chat!

As part of your Advent group meeting, you may care to talk about the contemporary implications of Isaiah's great 'Swords into Ploughshares' prophecy! 'They will beat their swords into ploughshares and their spears into pruning hooks. Nation will not take up sword against nation, nor will they train for war any more' (Isa. 2:4).

During an average year our government subsidises the arms trade to the tune of about £420 million. The money is largely channelled through the Export Credit Guarantee Department and the Defence Export Services Organisation. Neither of these organisations are directly accountable to the electorate and little is known about them. Unlike many industries, the arms trade can only function with government help. They must acquire licences for the export of arms, and the government often becomes involved in brokering deals for UK-based companies.

According to one report over 80 per cent of war victims are civilians and at least half of these are children. Very often, those wounded or killed in regional conflicts are the poor and marginalised. The very purchase of these armaments by their governments has taken money away from more urgent necessities of development and health-care.

● Should we ask serious questions about the way in which our taxes are spent?
● Wouldn't the world be a better place if there were more ploughshares and pruning hooks than tanks and attack-helicopters?
● Do you think that Christians should actively oppose the international arms trade as part of our vision of a 'new kingdom'?

John's Journey

8 DEC

Silenced by eternity

John's journey began before he was born! God had plans that John would fulfil – plans that had originated from the start of all things. Advent is a time for awe and wonder. The mystery of it all should render us speechless for it's all about God's action – not ours!

The Word

Throughout this week we'll be following the story of John the Baptist, another of the key Advent figures. Our journey begins with the angel's visit to Zechariah during his time of priestly duty in the Temple.

There are three significant things about the angel's prophecy which we should note. Firstly, John will bring many of the people of Israel back to the Lord, secondly he will go before the Lord as a kind of forerunner or preparer of the way and, finally, he will demonstrate the 'spirit and power of Elijah'. The Old Testament prophet Malachi prophesied that God would send the prophet Elijah 'before that great and dreadful day of the LORD comes. He will turn the hearts of the fathers to their children, and the hearts of the children to their fathers; or else I will come and strike the land with a curse' (Mal. 4:5–6).

The mystery of the angel's message is too much for Zechariah to take in. He is old, and his wife is 'well on in years' – the prospect of a baby at their time of life is more than he can cope with!

Read: Luke 1:5–25.

It is clear that God is at work, and that His plans supersede anything which Zechariah had ever dreamed of! As a result of his incredulity, Zechariah is made dumb, and he has to face the crowd with nothing to say. In the face of God's activity he is simply speechless!

Pause for thought

On this eighth step of our Advent journey we stand beside Zechariah, in a place which is far beyond his comfort zone! God's purposes are beyond the thinking of mortal men and women.

This 'God-event' had been prophesied for centuries. God is working His purposes out and, as promised, He is sending a forerunner to call the people to repentance, and to prepare the way of the Lord!

We can become so familiar with the Christmas story that we spend no time being just 'lost for words'. Part of the Advent journey is being dumbfounded, speechless and 'gobsmacked'!

It's allowing the majesty, the infinity, the eternity, of God's immeasurable plans to overwhelm us.

It's time for reason to be set aside, and to wonder at the awesome wisdom of God!

> **Read again: Luke 1:16–19.**

Punch line

The great Swiss theologian Karl Barth once wrote these words as a reflection on Zechariah's speechlessness:

> We must once and for all give up trying to be self-made individuals. Let us cease preaching by ourselves, being right by ourselves, doing good by ourselves, being sensible by ourselves, improving the world by ourselves. God wants to do everything, certainly through us and with us and never without us, but our participation in what he does must naturally originate and grow out of his power, not ours. O, how we could then speak with one another. For whatever does not grow out of God produces smoke, not fire. But that which is born of God overcomes the world.[1]

This is the message of Advent. Finding our place in what God has done, is doing and will do!

A time to pray
Take some space to savour the mystery of God's plan, devised before the dawn of creation, and stop trying to understand it all, grasp it all or bring it within your own sphere of reason.

Almighty and Everlasting God,
Your ways are higher than mine,
Your thoughts wiser that anything I can understand,
Your purposes span the great horizon of history,
Your plans supersede the ambitions of each and every one of us.

Thank You for silencing our worldly wisdom,
with a story so simple,
yet so compelling.
So basic,
yet so complex.
So earthy,
yet so full of heaven ...
that we can do no other but stand in awe.
Silenced by the wisdom of eternity.

Pray for others
For those who think too much, and listen too little.
Who argue about belief, and do not know the joy of faith.
Who speak much, but who have not learnt the silence of mystery.

Reflect or discuss
● What was Zechariah's experience in the Temple really like? Track the thoughts and emotions that must have flooded his mind while he was in that sacred space.
● Have you ever experienced a time in worship, prayer or Christian devotion when you glimpsed something greater than you'd ever imagined? What was it like?
● Look at Karl Bath's reflection on the Zechariah story. Do you agree with what he says?

● Are there ways in which we try to make God fit our plans instead of discovering how we fit His?
● Are we more focused on our doing rather than His doing through us?
● How can we change our lives this Advent?

9 DEC

The touch of God

In our Advent journey we reach the wonderful day of John the Baptist's birth. We discover that 'the Lord's hand was with him' and we ask how the Lord's hand might be with us.

The Word
The mysterious and wonderful story of John's arrival in the world enables the people to see that 'the Lord's hand is with him'. Zechariah, having regained his power of speech brings a beautifully prophetic word about the One who is soon to come. His song, which is often called 'The Benedictus' (from the opening word of the Latin translation of the text), describes the new hope of salvation for all the people.

Read: Luke 1:57–75.

Zechariah's long years as a priest and his lifetime of experience in the Temple make this prophecy all the more remarkable. His prophecy demonstrated that the Messiah would fulfil three great hopes of the people of Israel.

Firstly, that God would indeed 'come'. The word used for 'come' (v.68) was a military term; it was used when a captain visited his troops. The long-awaited Messiah was to be exactly this, God, coming on earth to see things for Himself 'first-hand'.

Secondly, that God would 'save'. The horn (v.69) is the strongest part of an animal; it's used for attack and defence and is at the core of the animal's life. The Messiah is the 'horn of salvation' and uses the axis of God's strength in His life and ministry. The long-awaited

Messiah would save the people.

Thirdly, that God would 'remember' (v.72). The Messiah was a symbol of God's ancient promises to Abraham, and of the covenant He had made with the people of Israel. The Messiah's arrival was a sign that God had not forgotten, nor had He stopped loving His people Israel!

John's role in 'preparing the people' for all these great promises to be fulfilled was very significant. It's little wonder, then, that 'the Lord's hand was with him' (v.66).

Pause for thought

Even on the day of his birth God had great plans for John! As these great and historic promises were about to be fulfilled, God needed someone to get things ready! The fact that the Lord's hand was with him from birth implies that God would constantly be guiding him and directing him – and that John would be responsive to God's tug!

Neil Hood, writing in *Whose Life is it Anyway?* recognised the importance of being responsive to God's touch.

Most busy people find it difficult to stop and take stock. In fact, excessive and apparently justifiable activity is a real hindrance to good stewardship. I recall how, as a young child, I used to be taken to the home of a very keen gardener who specialised in 'sensitive' plants (as he described them to me in a non-technical way). I found great entertainment in touching the leaves, and watching them respond as if by magic. Good stewardship is not a question of entertainment or magic, but it certainly is a response to the Lord's touch. So, in order to be good stewards we need to pause, take stock, and be obedient to God's touch in our lives. [2]

Punch line

In a real sense the Lord's hand is with each of us. He is constantly reaching out to us to support us, to guide us and to bless us. He has a ministry for all of us, and if we are responsive to the hand of God He will lead us into it.

John Stott wrote: 'In the scriptural sense "vocation has a broad and noble connotation" – its emphasis is not on the human (what we do) but on the divine (what God has called us to do).' [3]

A time to pray

Open our eyes wide, Lord,
to see the way ahead:
the dark dangers,
the hair-pin bends,
the hidden junctions,
the unexpected pit-falls
on this narrow road.

Open our eyes wide, Lord,
to see the way ahead:
the route to glory,
the path to heaven,
the road to holiness,
the track to sacrifice
on this narrow road.

Open our eyes wide, Lord,
to see the way ahead.
Deflect us from traps,
direct us from snares,
drive us past testings,
steer us past seductions,
turn us from temptations
on this narrow road.

Open our eyes wide, Lord
to see the way ahead.
Stretch out Your hand to guide us,
stretch out Your hand to support us,
stretch out Your hand to bless us ...
And lead us not into temptation,
but deliver us from evil
on this narrow road ...

Rob Frost

Pray for others
For those who are confused about their future direction ... That God may guide ...

Reflect or discuss
- Do you think that John's life was all set out before him ... or did he have real choices?
- In which way has God's hand been 'on your life'?
- Read again the quote from John Stott. Do we sometimes put the emphasis on what we want to do rather than on what God has called us to do?
- What happens when we miss God's best plan for our lives?

10 DEC

Preparing the way

John's role was that of preparing the way for Jesus in his day and generation. Each of us is commissioned to do the same in ours. The Advent journey is about preparing ourselves to receive the Lord Jesus at the great feast of Christmas. It's about getting right with God, and about being really open to His coming.

The Word
John goes before the Lord to help people to prepare for His coming by turning away from evil and by receiving forgiveness for their sins. His role was to prepare individuals and to get the whole nation ready so that they might receive Christ, and the salvation that He would usher in.

Read: Luke 1:76–79.

Pause for thought
The time before the arrival of a new baby can be a hectic period. Couples often decorate a nursery, attend pre-natal classes and spend large sums of money on baby clothes. Beyond all of this practical activity, however, there's a mental and emotional preparation

process, too. The new parents are already anticipating the great event and imagining how their lives will change when the new member of their family finally arrives.

Advent is a season in which we join John in the task of 'preparing the way of the Lord'. In some ways it's about working in the world to make it fit for the return of Jesus Christ. In other ways it's about our personal preparation for meeting Jesus when He comes back.

Punch line

Are you willing to 'prepare the way of the Lord' in your own life in the coming days of Advent? Are you willing to make this Advent season really count for God? Such an openness may lead to significant personal change.

A time to pray

There are many different kinds of prayer, and many disciplines to be learnt and developed.

As we begin to 'prepare the way of the Lord', may I invite you to take a journey 'inward'? Choose one or two of the roles you play in life …

Son or daughter   Mother or father
Brother or sister   Husband or wife
Employee or employer

Write down some of the ways in which you live that role; eg if you are a father you might identify worker, provider, protector or disciplinarian! Over the next 24 hours place this role before the Lord, and reflect on how you are living it in the midst of the everyday pressures of life. Again and again over the day reflect on your life in this role and pray …

'Lord, help me to be true to You and real with others.'

Pray for others

For those for whom you have some responsibility …

Reflect or discuss

● Why do you think that God sent John the Baptist ahead of Jesus?

What did John actually *do*?
- Is the Advent discipline of 'preparing for Jesus' just something internal and spiritual, or is it also about living life in the real world?
- Are there ways in which you end up 'playing a role' in everyday life like an actor on a stage? Talk about these different roles you play.
- Are you willing to make this Advent season really count for God?
- What does it actually mean to 'live like Jesus'?

11 DEC

Changing your mind!

John's message was one of repentance and of 'getting ready for God'. On our own Advent journey we pause today to get ourselves ready for the coming King.

The Word

Many years have slipped by since Zechariah heard from the angel in the Temple. John is now a grown man, and the prophecies pointing towards his future ministry are slowly coming true. It's important to remember that he was still proclaiming an 'Old Testament' gospel, and was very much functioning like an Old Testament prophet. God's unmerited love for sinners and His 'amazing grace' expressed on the cross were not yet part of the message! John had an important part to play in calling people to get right with God, however, as he prepared for the arrival of God's Son and the new kingdom which was approaching so fast.

Note that both John and Elijah dressed in a garment of hair garment with a leather belt; and both saw their mission as that of calling everyone to repentance.

Read: Matthew 3:1–12.

At the core of John's message was the challenge to 'change direction', 'turn back' and 'change your mind'. His Advent message was a stern warning to people to stop going their own way and to start going God's way!

Pause for thought

The tenth step of our Advent journey is a difficult step to take. It's a step of repentance, of 'changing direction' and of 'changing your mind'.

John reserved his harshest and sternest warnings for the most religious people in his audience. He explained that their religious heritage in Abraham did not exempt them from living a fruitful life. His words echo down the centuries to warn us, too. Our religious traditions, institutions, positions or rituals are not enough, of themselves, to save us. God looks beyond all that stuff into our lives and the attitudes and motives of our hearts. John warned that the Saviour would come one day to separate the wheat from the chaff. He will not only baptise with the Holy Spirit, but also with the fire of judgment. It's a real warning about how we should live our lives.

Advent gives us a special opportunity at the close of the year to 'repent', to 'change our minds' and to 'change direction'. As the remaining days of the old year ebb away and the new possibilities of a fresh beginning approach we can turn our regrets into new possibilities.

Repentance is far more than a recitation of past sins, or the repetitive ritual of 'prayers of confession'. It's about turning from one way of living to another. It's about leaving one lifestyle and adopting another. It's about saying sorry for what has gone and seeking to live a God-centred life.

> **Read again: Matthew 3:11–12.**

Punch line

Thomas à Kempis lived from 1380 to 1471. He was born in poverty near Cologne; became an Augustinian monk and wrote many powerful Christian mystical works. He wrote much on the theme of repentance and the importance of our preparedness to meet the Lord. The 1613 translation of his *The Imitation of Christ* reads:

In all things have a special aim to thy end, and how thou wilt be able to stand before that severe Judge to whom nothing is hid, who is not pacified with gifts, nor admitteth any excuses, but will judge according to right and equity.

O wretched and foolish sinner, who sometimes, fearest the countenance of an angry man, what answer wilt thou make to God who knoweth all thy wickedness.

Why dost thou provide for thyself against that great day of judgement, when no man can excuse or answer for another, but every one shall have enough to answer for himself!

Now are thy pains profitable, thy tears acceptable, thy groans audible, thy grief pacifieth God, and purgeth thy soul.[4]

A time to pray

Personal repentance is a central discipline for the season of Advent. This can't be done properly in a hurry – it demands unscrupulous personal honesty, reappraisal, saying sorry and a willingness to live a different life.

Spend time laying your life before God.
Allow Him to speak to you about your life.
Say sorry.
Lay yourself open to change from the inside … out!

Pray for others

For those who knowingly or unknowingly may have hurt you.
Seek to forgive them and ask God to help restore you to them.

Reflect or discuss

● Read again the words of Thomas à Kempis.
  Are they relevant today?
  Which phrases do you find most helpful?
● Matthew 3:12 says: 'His winnowing fork is in his hand, and he will clear his threshing-floor, gathering his wheat into the barn and burning up the chaff with unquenchable fire.'
  Explore this powerful image. What does it mean?
● Do you live as though God will judge you?
● Do you live in fear of judgment?

12 DEC

Recognising Jesus

Advent is a time for reviewing the great promises of the prophets and for recognising again who Jesus really is.

The Word

And so we reach the scene in John's story when we get to see John and Jesus in the same place at the same time!

John was using the popular Jewish symbol of baptism. This involved immersion in water, and was used to signify that a Gentile had converted to Judaism. Baptism symbolised their cleansing from the impurity of idolatry and their new birth. It was an important symbol of repentance.

What must have shocked everyone was that John was using baptism as a religious ceremony for *the Jews* – not the Gentiles! Through it John was saying that the Jews needed to repent and to be 'new-born'.

Read: Matthew 3:13–17.

Jesus was baptised to identify with the sinners whom He had come to save. He was also affirming John's ministry in encouraging people to repent and to 'change their ways'.

From the moment John saw Jesus he knew that this was someone who was very different. Someone set apart. He saw the Spirit descending in the form of a dove, and he heard God's public declaration about His Son.

Pause for thought

On this next step of our Advent journey we stand on the banks of the River Jordan with John the Baptist and wonder at the mystery of the One whom God has sent. Right from the announcement of His birth, God had made it clear that Jesus would be no ordinary man. The nature of His birth marked Him out as different and indicated that He was to be seen as the Son of God and not the son of Joseph.

While many people today can believe that Jesus was a great

prophet, teacher or healer, they cannot accept that He was and is, the Son of God. Without appreciating this, however, they haven't begun to comprehend who He really is. The Early Church was so concerned that its members should believe in Jesus' divine Sonship that they made it a basic confession for baptism. Mark introduced his Gospel with the words, 'The beginning of the gospel of Jesus Christ, the Son of God' (Mark 1:1).

In the Acts of the Apostles, Philip the evangelist made it clear to the Ethiopian eunuch that if he believed with all his heart, he could be baptised. The Ethiopian replied, 'I believe that Jesus Christ is the Son of God.'

Belief in Jesus as God's Son is one of the non-negotiable aspects of becoming a committed Christian.

Punch line

Today our recognition of Jesus as the Son of God will be under greater threat than ever. In a multi-cultural and multi-faith society there is growing pressure to build bridges with those who cannot accept that Jesus is the Son of God.

We should welcome dialogue with other faith communities, but there are some aspects of our faith which are non-negotiable. Our belief in Jesus as the Son of God is one of them. We may be considered bigoted and narrow, but it is at the core of our faith. It marks out Jesus' relationship with God as different from that of everyone else who ever lived.

It is this Sonship which gave Him the authority to say what He said and to do what He did and give us what He gave. This is a central tenet of our faith, and we shouldn't accept it lightly or easily. After all, we may be called upon to die rather than deny it.

A time to pray

We use as a focus for our meditation an excerpt from John Milton's classic poem *Paradise Regained*:

And he himself among them was baptized –
Not thence to be more pure, but to receive
The testimony of Heaven, that who he is
Thenceforth the nations may not doubt. I saw

The Prophet do him reverence; on him, rising
Out of the water, Heaven above the clouds
Unfold her crystal doors; thence on his head
A perfect Dove descend (whate'er it meant);
And out of Heaven the sovereign voice I heard,
'This is my Son beloved – in him am pleased.'
His mother, than, is mortal, but his Sire
He who obtains the monarchy of Heaven;
And what will He not do to advance his Son?
His first-begot we know, and sore have felt,
When his fierce thunder drove us to the Deep;
Who this is we must learn, for Man he seems
In all his lineaments, though in his face
The glimpses of his Father's glory shine.

Pray for others

Remember those today who languish in prisons around the world because they refuse to deny that Jesus is the *Son of God*.

Reflect or discuss

- Do you think that John the Baptist was popular or unpopular in his day?
- We skip forward to the end of John's story. Read together Matthew 14:6–12. What effect do you think John's death had on his disciples?
- Do you think people are tolerant of really committed Christians today?
- Have you ever experienced intolerance towards your faith or witness? How did it feel?

13 DEC

The coming Saviour

Our journey today takes us to a prison cell – and to John's struggle in faith to know what the Messiah would be like. Advent is a time for us to focus on Jesus' ministry as Saviour and to understand what that really means.

The Word

John was in prison because he had upset King Herod and had dared to challenge him about aspects of his personal life. Whilst there he struggled with the news he heard about Jesus. So he sent his disciples to check Him out, and to ask the question, 'Are you the one who was to come, or should we expect someone else?' (Matt. 11:3).

Earlier, in Matthew 3, we read how John preached about 'the one who is to come after me' but his question here implies that he was having second thoughts! The kind of Messiah whom John was expecting was very much the Judge who would pursue the destruction of the wicked.

Jesus sends the messengers back to John with news of His ministry about the blind seeing, the lame walking, the lepers being healed, the deaf who can hear and the dead who are alive! He's drawing on the kind of Messianic vision which Isaiah described in Isaiah 29:18–19; 35:5–6; 61:1. In His reply Jesus reminds John that as the 'Suffering Servant' He has not come to destroy as much as to restore, to save and to heal!

Read: Matthew 11:2–19.

Pause for thought

Jesus mixed with outcasts, sinners, prostitutes and traitors, because these were the very people who recognised their need of a Saviour! He taught that it's not the healthy who need a doctor, but those who recognise that they are sick!

The Bible teaches that Jesus did not come to humiliate us or to disgrace us, but to rescue us. When the angel announced the arrival of a Saviour, he was declaring the good news that Christ had not come on earth to condemn us but to rescue us, to find us and to save us.

Those who think they can save themselves by their religious duty, their good works in the world or their 'nice' demeanour are much mistaken. Jesus came into the world as Saviour because He came to do what we can never do. He came to bring us back into relationship with God, to forgive us our sins and to set us off in a new direction. In the wonderful stories of the woman who lost her precious wedding coin, the shepherd who lost his sheep, and the father who lost his son, we get an insight into the kind of compassion and care that the Lord has for each of us.

Punch line

Christmas should be a joyful time! It's about the arrival of someone to rescue us, to save us, to set us free. 'For God so loved the world that he gave his one and only Son, that whoever believes in him shall not perish but have eternal life. For God did not send his Son into the world to condemn the world, but to save the world through him' (John 3:16–17).

No longer need we look to the future with despair or fear of judgment. No longer need we carry the burden of guilt and failure. For God has sent us a Saviour! We can ask Him to save us and to forgive us and to bring us into a new relationship with God.

A time to pray

As we think of the saving grace of Jesus in our Advent prayers today, we use words first penned by the great Scottish hymnwriter Horatius Bonar (1808–1889). In his first parish, in Kelso, a servant in his home was converted through hearing his prayers through his locked study door.

Upon a Life I have not lived,
Upon a Death I did not die,
Another's Life, Another's Death;
I stake my whole eternity.

Not on the tears which I have shed;
Not on the sorrows I have known;
Another's tears; Another's griefs;
On them I rest, on them alone.

Jesus, O Son of God, I build
On what Thy cross has done for me;
There both my death and life I read;
My guilt, my pardon there I see.

Lord, I believe; O deal with me
As one who has Thy Word believed!

I take the gift, Lord, look on me
As one who has Thy gift received.

Pray for others
Pray for people by name among your family and friends who, as yet, don't know Jesus as their personal Saviour.

Reflect or discuss
● What kind of stories about Jesus do you think that John was receiving in his prison cell? Why did he struggle with them?
● What kind of things do you think John had been expecting Jesus to do?
● What was Jesus' first priority?
● In an age in which we are supposed to be all coping, self-sufficient and dependent on nobody, what does it mean to be 'saved'?

14 DEC

Sender and sent

As we conclude the story of John the Baptist and the second week of our Advent journey, we look at John's important role as someone sent by God.

The Word
In the opening verses of John's Gospel we see the strategic place which John the Baptist held in God's perfect plan. He was sent as a 'witness to ... the light' (John 1:7).

The Greek word for witness, *martur*, gives us the English 'martyr' – someone who is willing to bear witness even though it costs his or her life. It turned out to be a very appropriate title for John.

Many thought that John the Baptist would fulfil all of Israel's hopes, but every time we read about him he is always 'witnessing' that it is Jesus who will do this, not him. Again and again the religious authorities, the priests and Levites, ask John who he really is. He tells them that he is not the Christ, he is not Elijah, and he is not a prophet like Moses. He is simply the one who has been sent to prepare the way!

Read: John 1:1–23.

Pause for thought

Expectations were high, and John seemed to fit the image of the kind of Messiah many were expecting, but he steadfastly refused to move beyond his calling.

John's ministry was not an easy one. He had to call people to repentance, remind the religious activists that they needed to get right with God, and challenge the power brokers of his day to live for God. It was tough and challenging work and, in the end, it cost him his life.

Punch line

We read in John 1 that John the Baptist 'came as a witness to testify concerning that light, so that through him all men might believe'.

> **Every Christian shares this calling. Are you a 'witness to the light'?**

Talkabout

If you are in a group, you could use the 'Reflect or discuss' sections from the last six days as a basis for discussion.

Meditation

On this fourteenth day of our Advent journey we pause to meditate.

You may like to light the second advent candle in a darkened room, play some Christmas music on the stereo, and read our second Advent meditation by candlelight.

Pause to think about what you have learnt and felt during the last six days of these studies.

At the close of our Advent journey with John we're going to focus on the mystery of Christ's coming.

A view from the Universe

Jim Lovell, the Apollo astronaut, described our planet from space as 'whole and round and beautiful and small. It was just another body, really, about four times bigger than the moon. But it held all the hope and all the life and all the things that the crew of Apollo 8 knew and loved. It was the most beautiful thing there was to see in all the heavens.'

James Shepherd, who walked on the moon said, 'It was more significant that God walked on the earth than that man walked on the moon ...'

Rick Warren once wrote:

You see, if God had wanted to communicate to cows, He would have become a cow. If God had wanted to communicate to ants, He would have become an ant. If God had wanted to communicate to dogs, He would have become a dog. But he wanted to communicate to human beings, so He became one of us, a human being. Now I can look at Jesus and say, 'Oh that's how God wants me to live. That's what God is like.'[5]

Prayer Link

Lord of the universe,
You stride among the galaxies,
And view the endless train of planets
Shining to infinity.
Yet one tiny light,
Tinged with blue,
Stands out from all the rest.
For this was home to You
The day You left Your paradise.
Traded Your cloak of stars
For a wooden cross,
Exchanged power for powerlessness,
Heaven for earth,
Bliss for pain.
Remember us, this day ...

And give us our daily bread ...
That we might have enough ...
And to share ...[6]

Rob Frost

Coffee and chat

As part of your Advent group meeting, you may care to talk about
the implications of 'defending the faith' in the light of what
happened to John the Baptist.

John the Baptist lived in an age when, if you offended the
authorities, you could lose your head! Some believe that Christians
who hold strong views about the right to believe, the right to belong
and the right to proclaim are, like John the Baptist, in danger of
offending people in an increasingly intolerant and politically correct
society.

In a debate about counter terrorism after 9/11, Mr Blunkett, the
Home Secretary, said (*Hansard* Column 36), 'The argument is not
whether people should be allowed to say what they want but
whether the intention, and the likely effect, of their comments is
to stir up racial hatred ...'

This seems a very politically correct and well-intentioned kind of
statement, but in the same debate Sir Brian Mawhinny pointed out
the flaw in the argument.

Sir Brian said, 'The Home Secretary will know, to use his own
words, that two of the central foundations of the Christian faith –
namely, that Jesus Christ was both man and God and that people
can get into a relationship with God only through Jesus Christ – are
deemed by some in other religions to be insulting and offensive.
Indeed, in some countries it is so insulting and offensive that the
very statement of Christian faith is enough to put someone in
prison ...'

Sir Brian has summed up the concerns of many. The politically
correct among us seem to be advocating a bland multi-faith
approach to life, but this is simply incompatible with a kind of
Christianity which sees the upholding of core tenets of faith and
the importance of evangelism as a central part of its practice.

This rising tide of political correctness may threaten the rights of
Christians to share their faith, to nominate 'doctrinally sound' leaders

to Christian organisations and to employ Christians in key roles in the life of the church.

Yet Article 9 of the European Convention on Human Rights gives all religions the inherent legal right to propagate their faith.

Yet Section 43 of the Education Act of 1986 gives religious groups protection to evangelise because it is a form of freedom of speech.

Yet Human Rights Law, recognises the principle of 'Freedom of Association'. It teaches that one of those rights is to exclude people from our organisations if they do not subscribe to our fundamental principles.

And the Magna Carta of 1215 reads: 'We have confirmed for us and our heirs in perpetuity that the English Church shall be free and shall have its right undiminished and its liberty unimpaired ...'

> **Do you believe that there is a growing intolerance to Christian belief, practice and proclamation? If so, what should we do about it?**

---

1. Karl Barth, *Lukas 1-5-23, Predigten 1917*, pp.423–431. Copyright © Theologischer Verlag Zurich 1999. Translated by Robert J. Sherman.

2. Neil Hood, *Whose Life is it Anyway?* (Carlisle: Authentic Lifestyle, 2002).

3. John Stott, *The Contemporary Christian* (Leicester: IVP, 1992).

4. *The Imitation of Christ*, Thomas à Kempis (Oxford: first pub in The World's Classics Series in 1903).

5. Rick Warren, *The Heart of Christmas* (Nashville: Thomas Nelson Publishers, 1998).

6. Rob Frost, *Hopes and Dreams* (Eastbourne: Kingsway Communications Ltd, 1999).

Mary's Journey

15 DEC

Making space

In this third week of our Advent pilgrimage we journey with Mary, the mother of Jesus, and learn things from her story which will help us to live out our story.

The Word

The amazing news of the Incarnation was brought to Mary by Gabriel. He is one of only three angels whose names we are given in the Bible – he appears four times, and always bringing good news (Dan. 8:16; 9:21; Luke 1:19; 26). When we read of him in the book of Daniel we discover that he warns that sin is a reality and one day must be paid for. He explains to Daniel that the Messiah will have to 'be cut off' in order for this to happen. ('After the sixty-two "sevens', the Anointed One will be cut off and will have nothing', Dan. 9:26.)

Centuries later, the angel Gabriel returns again with more news about the Messiah, for the time has finally arrived for the fulfilment of God's great plan of salvation. Gabriel tells Mary that Jesus will be the Son of the Highest, that He will inherit the throne of His forefather David, that He will reign over the house of Jacob forever, and that He will have an everlasting kingdom.

Read: Luke 1:26–38.

Pause for thought

In this mysterious Advent story we see how Mary responds to

Gabriel's challenging message. She can relate to his message because she has some knowledge of the prophets and the Jewish teaching with which she has grown up. But it's a message which invites a response and the whole of eternity rests on the choice that she makes.

Punch line

Mary takes hold of God's promise and makes it her own. The Virgin Mary is not just a passive participant in God's plan of salvation; she makes a decision, she believes and she obeys. In Latin the root of the word 'conceive' means to 'seize, or take hold of'. Of all the different characters in the Advent story Mary offers the most precious gift of all. She offers a womb, a place of safety and nourishment. It is a response of limitless belief and love.

Our response to Jesus doesn't begin with 'doing', it's about making space at the core of who we are so that He will come and 'dwell with us'.

> **Have you 'made room for Jesus' in your life?**

A time to pray

Dear Lord and heavenly Father,
I recognise that, without Jesus, I can do nothing:
that all fruitfulness starts with Him.
That I must abide in Him.
That He might abide in me.
For without Him I am powerless.

Lord, I need to make space for Jesus.
To focus less on what I do for Him ...
And more on who I am in Him.

Help me make more room for Him.
Help me to live in Him that He may live in me.
Amen.

Pray for others
Pray for mothers. We remember our own mothers before God.

Reflect or discuss
- Do you believe in angels?
- Have you ever had an experience of an angel?
- Imagine what the angel's news meant for Mary.
  What emotions would have overwhelmed her?
  What would have been the toughest situations
  facing her?
- What does it mean practically to 'make room for Jesus' in your life?

16 DEC

The joy of the Lord

Advent should be pure joy: joy at the fulfilment of God's promises; joy at the arrival of the long-expected Messiah; joy for the difference He makes in all lives.

The Word
Three people are caught up in a great expression of joy in our reading today. First, there is the joy of the unborn baby, John the Baptist, who 'leaped' in his mother's womb at the arrival of Mary. Then there was the joy Elizabeth felt when she heard Mary's greeting and 'was filled with the Holy Spirit'. Finally, there was the joy of Mary, whose beautiful song 'The Magnificat' resonates with good news for all.

Read: Luke 1:39–49.

Pause for thought
The theme of joy runs throughout the whole of Scripture. Abraham rejoiced in God's promise to him. David was joyful because he knew that the Saviour would be descended from him. Isaiah was filled with joy when he thought about the coming kingdom. The psalms are laced with joy. Paul was full of joy over the progress of churches

in Corinth, Philippi and Thessalonica.

Jesus linked prayer to joy when He said: 'Until now you have not asked for anything in my name. Ask and you will receive, and your joy will be complete' (John 16:24).

Punch line

Professor F.F. Bruce used to say, 'Peace is joy resting, joy is peace dancing.' Both emotions emanate from a life dedicated to God and a right relationship with Jesus Christ. If we are 'out of step' in our walk with Jesus, our personal sense of joy and peace are the first things to go.

Joy is a fruit of the Holy Spirit's life within us (Gal. 5:22). Joy is very different from happiness! It does not depend on circumstances, on 'everything going to plan', or on an easy or prosperous life. Joy stems from a living relationship with God, and the strengthening and comforting presence of the Holy Spirit in our lives.

A time to pray

Today we use a Christmas carol as the focus of our prayer. The words were written by Isaac Watts, whose childhood was not easy because his father was imprisoned twice for his religious views. Isaac learned Greek, Latin and Hebrew under Mr Pinhorn, a rector and headmaster in Southampton. Isaac's ability to write in verse was evident from early childhood. He wrote most of his *Hymns and Spiritual Songs* between the ages of 20 and 22 years.

Joy to the world, the Lord is come!
Let earth receive her King;
Let every heart prepare Him room,
And heaven and nature sing,
And heaven and nature sing,
And heaven, and heaven, and nature sing.

Joy to the world, the Saviour reigns!
Let men their songs employ;
While fields and floods, rocks, hills and plains
Repeat the sounding joy,
Repeat the sounding joy,
Repeat, repeat, the sounding joy.

No more let sins and sorrows grow,
Nor thorns infest the ground;
He comes to make His blessings flow
Far as the curse is found,
Far as the curse is found,
Far as, far as, the curse is found.

He rules the world with truth and grace,
And makes the nations prove
The glories of His righteousness,
And wonders of His love,
And wonders of His love,
And wonders, wonders, of His love.

Pray for others

John, the unborn child, features strongly in today's reading. Even in the womb he responds to news of the coming Saviour!

- We pray today for those who are expecting children, and for those considering abortion as an option.
- We remember those who work politically and in public life to change the laws on abortion.
- We remember, with sadness, the six million new lives terminated since the abortion laws were changed in the UK.

Reflect or discuss

- What makes you happy and what makes you joyful?
- What kind of relationship do you think that Mary and Elizabeth shared?
- Is it possible to 'lose your joy' as a Christian? If so, how do you get it back?

17 DEC

A radical challenge

Today's Advent material reminds us that this season is not only a time for introspection and reflection but it's also a time for practical action. God stands on the side of the poor, the humble and the oppressed, and He calls us to stand there too.

The Word

Mary's beautiful song, the Magnificat, reminds us of God's great faithfulness, and speaks of His mercy and favour towards those who are the 'little people' of society. The humble, the weak and the voiceless.

Very often we picture Mary as a quiet, obedient servant of God who is content to remain in the background. She came from a humble background and is often characterised as 'meek and mild'. The Magnificat demonstrates that there was much more to Mary than we often imagine! Her God-inspired words are raw and radical. They are words of revolution!

She underscores the righteous anger of the prophets of old. She declares that the era to come will see a time when many of the old ideas about power, prestige and prosperity are overturned. Those who think that God sides with the powerful must think again, for God actually stands alongside those who have nothing. Mary may sound a bit like a radical revolutionary but she is actually pinpointing many of the themes which will feature in Jesus' coming ministry.

Read: Luke 1:50–56.

Pause for thought

When Jesus announced that the 'kingdom of God' was near, He made it clear that God's kingdom would mean good news for the poor but bad news for the proud and the rich. He said:

'The Spirit of the Lord is on me, because he has anointed me to preach good news to the poor. He has sent me to proclaim freedom for the prisoners and recovery of sight for the blind, to release the oppressed, to proclaim the year of the Lord's favour' (Luke 4:18–19).

We live in a world in which power, money and fame count for much. We need to recognise that God's values are very different from those which dominate our culture!

Punch line

Advent is a time to prepare for the return of Christ and the consummation of all things in His kingdom. It's a time to recognise that each of us has a part to play in ushering in that kingdom and in standing up for its values. Patrick Dixon once wrote:

When acts of kindness are carried out by believers, the love of God is seen. This is an aggressive act, giving power and substance to the message we proclaim. We care because people are worth it, made in the image of God. We care not for results or reward, but because God calls us to care, and because when God has touched our lives we find we can respond in no other way to human need.[1]

A time to pray

Oscar Romero who fought for the rights of the poor in South America and who was killed in the midst of his prophetic ministry recognised that we don't only need to stand with the poor ... but to recognise our own poverty of spirit.

No-one can celebrate a genuine Christmas without
  being spiritually poor.
The self-sufficient, the proud, those who, because they
  have everything, look down on others,
Those who have no need even of God – for them there
  will be no Christmas.
Only the poor, the hungry, those who need someone
  to come on their behalf, will have that someone.
That someone is God. Emmanuel. God-with-us.
Without poverty of spirit there can be no abundance
  of God.[2]

Lord, forgive me that I am so self-sufficient
               so easily satisfied
               so full of self.

Create in me an empathy with the poor, that I may truly
understand.
Create in me a poverty of spirit which reaches out to
You for more …

Pray for others
Think about those who are cold and homeless today.

Reflect or discuss
- What kind of person was Mary?
- Look at the Magnificat again. What does the world look like from God's point of view?
- What could we do, this Advent, to make a difference in the world?

18 DEC

God is with us

We walk with Mary through difficult days and learn that Advent is
about knowing that 'God is with us' all the time. It's a time to let
God into every aspect of our everyday lives.

The Word
Mary was betrothed to Joseph, and he was legally her husband even
before the marriage took place. The marriage was only complete,
however, when the bridegroom took the bride home and the
marriage was consummated.

There must have been some tough times for Mary during her
betrothal. In today's reading we learn of Joseph's doubts. He was
thinking about divorcing Mary. One can only imagine what this
would have meant for her in her culture.

Joseph was well within his rights to break off the relationship.
A Jewish betrothal could be dissolved if the man gave the woman
a written document of divorce. It was a serious matter however,
because in this culture a betrothed girl was considered to be a widow
if her fiancé died. 'Betrothal' therefore represented a far more serious
level of commitment than our modern custom of 'engagement'.

These, then, were uncertain days for Mary. Which would Joseph choose ... pride or obedience?

Read: Matthew 1:18–25.

Pause for thought

'Emmanuel' is a descriptive title which means 'God is with us'. It's a title which many of us will come across in Bible readings and hymns around this time of year, but what does it mean for us today?

The coming of Jesus into the world in Bethlehem is all about God stepping into our human condition. He comes to be with us in whatever circumstances we find ourselves! Too often we only hunger for His presence when we're facing big needs, dark experiences or bad times. It's as though 'Emmanuel' only applies when we're in a tricky situation and desperately need help. This, however, is plainly not what 'Emmanuel' is supposed to mean! If we know Jesus as 'Emmanuel – God with us' it should apply to the whole of our lives, not just those times when we need some extra help!

When Jesus comes to us as Emmanuel, He comes to engage with all of who we are, not just carefully selected segments! In her days of uncertainty Mary must have drawn great strength from this understanding.

Punch line

Advent is a time to celebrate that 'Emmanuel – God is with us' in our troubles and traumas and in our temptations and failures. When Jesus came to earth to be our 'Emmanuel' He came to enter every part of our lives. He's even with us in those compartments of our lives which we've locked Him out of!

A time to pray

In the pressures of your everyday life you may care to find a quiet place. Sit down. Relax. Breathe in and out deeply.

As you breathe in, think, 'Christ is with me.'
As you hold your breath think, 'Christ is in me.'

As you breathe out think, 'Christ walks beside me.'
In all your meetings with people today, seek to 'be like
   Christ' to each person.
In all your meetings today seek to see Christ in those you meet.

Pray for others
Pray for friends, relatives or neighbours who are passing through
troubled times in their marriage.

Reflect or discuss
● What would have been the implications for Mary if Joseph had
   divorced her?
● What is it like to feel insecure?
   In a friendship?
   In a marriage?
   In the workplace?
● How do you cope with your own insecurities?
● How can God be 'our security'?
● How can we discover 'God with us' even in our insecurities?

19 DEC

Thy will be done

Mary's journey was to take her through many difficult experiences.
As we look to the future we ask God to help us to know His will
and to give us the grace to be obedient to it!

The Word
Mary carefully observed the birth ceremonies of the Jewish people.
Eight days after her baby was born He was circumcised and named
Jesus.

   About a month later, 40 days after His birth, Jesus was taken to the
Temple in Jerusalem to be dedicated to the Lord, as He was the first-
born male of the family. It was also the time when Mary offered a
sacrifice for her purification after giving birth. It's interesting to note
that the sacrifice was 'a pair of doves or two young pigeons'. This

was the humblest kind of sacrifice, and shows that this was a very poor family.

Two elderly people in the Temple recognise the significance of the moment, and the importance of Jesus' arrival.

Read: Luke 2:29–35.

Pause for thought

Simeon's prophetic word wasn't all good news. He recognised that God had provided salvation through Jesus, but he also saw that He would be very unpopular. The old man, speaking to Mary, continued, 'And a sword will pierce your own soul too.' Mary's journey with Jesus would be heartbreaking, painful. Yet it was part of God's call on her life.

God's call does not always mean that life will turn out to be a bed of roses. It can sometimes lead to great personal sacrifice and even heartbreak.

Punch line

As we follow Mary down the years we can see how Simeon's warning was fulfilled again and again. How did she feel when the boy Jesus disappeared in the Temple 'on His Father's business'? What was it like at the wedding in Cana when He told her, 'My hour has not come'? How did she feel when she heard the teachers of the law say that He was possessed? And what did she go through when, at last, she was with Him at the cross?

Mary's call was not simple and her journey was not easy. Everything that affected Jesus affected her. She seemed to embrace each new challenge as an opportunity to serve God. God's call may not always be easy, but it's always right.

A time to pray

Lord, I would hear You,
I would obey You.
I would know Your call on my life
and I would seek to fulfil it.

I do not ask for a comfortable life
nor do I ask for an easy one.
I ask for a life moulded to Your perfect plan.
Shaped for Your holy purposes.
Formed for what You made me to become.

I know that this will bring joy,
and sometimes it will bring sorrow.
Some days I will rejoice in Your plans for me,
and on others I will struggle to make sense of it all.

But here and now I lay my life before You,
and I say again,
'Thy will be done in me ...'

Pray for others
For those who are struggling with understanding God's will for
their lives.

Reflect or discuss
● Do you think that God has a plan and purpose for your life?
● Are you open to receive it and to obey it?
● Do you think that Mary and Joseph knew what was going to
  happen to their son?
● Has God ever brought a Simeon or an Anna into your life? Who
  was it? How did he or she help you on your journey?

20 DEC

The family of God

Mary's journey took her through some difficult times as a mother.
Advent is a time when we focus on the 'holy family', and Mary's role
in the family of Jesus. It's also a time for thinking about our own
families, and for grasping at the mystery of the 'family of God'.

The Word

Jesus had reached a very difficult phase of His ministry. There were massive expectations from the crowd following Him and life was so pressured that He couldn't even eat (Mark 3:20). The teachers of the law were accusing Him of using demonic power to achieve His miracles; the Pharisees were accusing Him of breaking the Sabbath. The heat was on and times were tough. The close members of His family were very concerned about Him, so they went to see Him. Mark tells us that they were saying, 'He is out of his mind' (Mark 3:21).

Read: Mark 3:31–35.

Pause for thought

This short passage raises more questions about Mary's involvement than it gives answers. Did Mary feel that her son was 'out of His mind'? Did she think His public ministry was 'taking a turn for the worse'? Did she question what He was doing because so many religious leaders were condemning Him? Was her son's overwhelming popularity with the crowd something she hadn't expected? Or, as His mother, was she just worried that He didn't even have time to eat; or, for the sake of family unity, was she eager to accompany them on their visit to Jesus to keep some control of the situation?

Whatever the truth, we can be assured that Mary was concerned about her son, and wanted to be with Him at a difficult time.

Punch line

There are two distinct groups of people evident in this scene. One group, His followers and disciples, are seated in a circle around Jesus. The other group, His close family, are standing outside.

Jesus makes it clear that He now has only one family. 'Whoever does God's will is my brother and sister and mother' (Mark 3:35). True and profound though His words were, they must have pierced Mary's heart.

Each of us is faced with this stark choice. Are we with Him or against Him? Part of the circle of those who do God's will … or the strangers hanging around outside?

A time to pray

Thomas à Kempis wrote *The Imitation of Christ* in the early fifteenth century. Its challenge is as fresh today as when it was first written. Use these words to think about your relationship with Jesus Christ. Are you with Him or against Him? Inside the family circle … or still outside?

What can the world profit thee without Jesus?
To be without Jesus is a grievous hell; and to be with
  Jesus, a sweet paradise.
If Jesus be with thee, no enemy shall be able to hurt
  thee.
He that findeth Jesus, findeth a good treasure, yea a
  Good above all good.
And he that loseth Jesus, loseth much indeed, yea more
  than the whole world!
Most poor is he who liveth without Jesus; and he most
  rich who is well with Jesus.[3]

Pray for others

● Remember the members of your own family, especially those who are going through difficult times.
● Pray for those who are in family crisis. Ask that God will be with them.

Reflect or discuss

● How do you think Mary felt about Jesus at this stage in His ministry?
● What kind of family did Jesus have in mind when He said, 'Here are my mother and my brothers!'?
● Is the Church a family to you?
● How can we develop a greater sense of the 'family of God' in the life of the Church?

21 DEC

A mother's grief

We have followed Mary's journey from Nazareth, and today we reach the final destination. We find her standing at the foot of the cross. The Advent season reminds us that the Messiah was to come as a suffering servant, that He would be 'cut off' and His stripes would bring healing to the nations. In our reading today we stand with Mary at the cross and see those ancient prophecies fulfilled.

The Word

Many scholars believe that the cross on which Jesus was crucified was not tall. At a crucifixion, then, the condemned person was very close, and soldiers would be guarding the prisoner in case anyone should try and take him down.

This must have been a harrowing experience for Mary as she stood only yards away from her son's broken body. Many believe that she was accompanied by her sister, the mother of James and John. If that is so, the John who was also standing there, would have been Jesus' cousin.

Crucifixion was a dark and terrible form of execution, and it must have been a dreadful experience to watch someone you love suffer in that way.

Read: John 19:23–27.

Pause for thought

Mary's journey with Jesus was nearly over. She had given birth in a borrowed stable. She had taken her newborn to Egypt as a refugee. She had seen Him criticised and condemned by the religious establishment. She had witnessed the hatred in her hometown of Nazareth – for the people there had wanted to kill Him. And so, under orders from the king and with the complicity of the Roman authorities and the high priest, He faces the final humiliation. He is crucified as a common criminal.

How Mary coped with this diverse array of painful memories is a mystery. Perhaps the wonderful things that she 'stored in her heart' from those early days of Jesus' life may have kept her going.

Punch line

Sometimes God's will is mysterious, unknowable and beyond our understanding. It's important to 'store in our hearts' those positive experiences of His guidance and grace, for we may need them to sustain us in more difficult days!

Talkabout

If you are in a group, you could use the 'Reflect or discuss' sections from the last six days as a basis for discussion.

Meditation

On this 21st day of our Advent journey we pause to meditate rather than to talk. You may like to light an Advent candle in a darkened room, play some Christmas music on the stereo, and read our third Advent meditation by candlelight!

Pause to think about what you have heard and felt about Mary's journey during the last six days.

For our meditation we are looking at the last verses of the old hymn, 'Christians awake, salute the happy morn'.

To Bethl'em straight the enlightened shepherds ran,
To see the wonder God had wrought for man:
Then to their flocks, still praising God, return,
And their glad hearts with holy rapture burn;
Amazed, the wondrous tidings they proclaim,
The first apostles of his infant fame.

Like Mary, let us ponder in our mind
God's wondrous love in saving lost mankind;
Trace we the Babe, who has retrieved our loss,
From his poor manger to his bitter cross;
Tread in his steps, assisted by his grace,
Till our first heavenly state again takes place.

Then may we hope, the angelic hosts among,
To sing, redeemed, a glad triumphal song;
He that was born upon this joyful day
Around us all his glory shall display;
Saved by his love, incessant we shall sing
Th' eternal praise of heaven's almighty King.

John Byrom (1692—1763) alt.

Coffee and chat

As part of your Advent group meeting, you may care to talk about the implications of Mary and Joseph's 'flight into Egypt'. When they ran in fear of Herod they went as asylum seekers to a foreign land.

Asylum has become an emotive and highly politicised issue in the United Kingdom. Just as Mary and Joseph took Jesus and ran for fear of Herod so thousands turn to Britain for fear of their lives each year. They look to us for help in a similar time of crisis. How can the Church become active in the asylum debate, what do we want to say, and how can we support and help those who arrive here from places of persecution or experiences of torture?

---

1. Patrick Dixon, *Out of the Ghetto and Into the City* (Milton Keynes: Word Books, 1995) p.33.

2. From an address Oscar Romero gave on 24 December 1978.

3. Thomas à Kempis, *The Imitation of Christ*. First edition in Latin, 1470.

Jesus' Journey

22 DEC

The Word of God

At the start of the fourth week of our Advent journey we think about the journey that Jesus made. The life of Jesus did not begin in a stable, but before the start of time itself. We do not worship a baby in a manger, but the Lord of all!

The Word

Mark starts the story of Jesus with His baptism, Matthew starts at Jesus' birth, and Luke goes even further back to the announcement of Zechariah. But John starts his Gospel in a different age. Before the start of time itself! He does not try to place Jesus in time or through ancestry; he says that Jesus existed 'in the beginning'. These words remind us of Genesis 1:1, 'In the beginning God …' and were probably a direct reference by John to the first book of the Hebrew Scriptures which was known as the 'In the beginning' book!

John goes back even further! The 'Word' who was with God before anything was made and from whom all light and life have come. John makes it clear that 'the Word' was with God and that 'the Word' was God. Jesus was not only pre-existent but an intimate part of the Godhead.

Read: John 1:1–14.

Pause for thought

It's good that Matthew sets the Jesus story in genealogy, so that we know the family roots from which He came. It's good that Luke gives us historical references so that we know that Jesus actually came in real time. But it's important that John sets Jesus in the context of eternity.

Punch line

Jesus is part of the God who was and is and is to come.

A time to pray

Today we use words written over 1,500 years ago as a theme for our meditation. They were written by St John Chrysostom, who has been called 'the greatest preacher in the early church'. He was born in 374 and died in 407. He grew up in Syrian Antioch in a Christian family. John was ordained as a priest in Antioch, where he served for 12 years before being made archbishop of Constantinople. His classical education proved of great benefit to his ministry, even if his linguistic education was limited to Greek. His writing is beautiful and poetic – his explanation of John 1 profound.

Truly wondrous is the whole chronicle of the nativity. For this day the ancient slavery is ended, the devil confounded, the demons take to flight, the power of death is broken. For this day paradise is unlocked, the curse is taken away, sin is removed, error driven out, truth has been brought back, the speech of kindliness diffused and spread on every side – a heavenly way of life has been implanted on the earth, angels communicate with men without fear, and we now hold speech with angels. Why is this? Because God is now on earth and man in heaven; on every side all things commingle. He has come on earth, while being fully in heaven; and while complete in heaven, he is without diminution on earth. Though he was God, he became man, not denying himself to be God. Though being the unchanging Word, he became flesh that he might dwell among us.

Pray for others

For those who are looking for spirituality, but who have not discovered or explored the Christian treasure store of deeply spiritual writings.

Reflect or discuss

● Look at St John Chrysostom's description. Are there parts you find confusing or that you don't understand?
● The One who sat on the throne came to lie in a manger. What did it really mean for Jesus to leave heaven to come to earth?
● How can we develop our Christian spirituality so that we can draw fully on the heritage of our faith?

23 DEC

Jesus holds it all together

It's easy to be so focused on the baby in the manger at this Christmas season that we forget just how powerful and majestic the Jesus of Eternity really is. The journey of Jesus started before the world began, and it continued through the work of creation at the beginning of all things. As we approach Christmas and the manger, we remember today the true significance of the Creator Jesus, our Lord and King.

The Word

Today's passage reminds us that Jesus is the One who holds everything together. He was the Creator force behind everything in heaven and on earth. He is eternal, and 'before all things' and so He holds history in His hand. He is the head of the Church. He was the Saviour, the 'first-born from the dead'.

The Body of Christ only works when it lives under the authority of the head. Lack of submission to the head leads to total paralysis. When members of the Body are not submitted to the head, they don't receive the right signals, they don't run in co-ordination with each other, and they're not submitted to the will of Him to whom the Body belongs.

One of the greatest contributions of the Celtic Christians to the richness of Christian spirituality is that they recognised Christ's immanence in the whole of life. They understood that Christ is not only over all, but that He is in all. His presence suffuses the whole of creation and fills every creative aspect of it.

Read: Colossians 1:15–20.

Pause for thought
In these special days of Advent, pause to gaze in wonder at the world around you. Even in dark wintry days it's remarkable just how much is happening in nature. Look at the scudding clouds, the rain or snow, pale sunshine breaking through and the starry winter sky. This Advent, look beyond all this to see the One who created it, and watch for His created glory.

Punch line
Jesus is the Lord of all things. He was present at the dawn of creation – and His creative power suffuses all that He has made.

A time to pray
Lord Jesus, I'm glad that You're not just an idea, or a myth, a philosophy or a proposition, a manifesto or a story. You came, seeable – touchable – hearable – historical – actual. The Word made flesh. God incarnate. A light in the darkness. A baby in a manger. My Saviour. Amen.

Lord, I hear the angels sing Your praises. Louder than the roar of a football crowd. Softer than the lap of the gentle wave. More harmonious than a choir. Less structured than the simplest melody. Glory, glory, glory. Glory to You in the highest, the King of kings. For ever and ever. Amen!

Pray for others
We pray for all who are concerned with caring for the world. We think of Christians committed to ecology and whose care for creation is a great witness to God's redeeming love.

Reflect or discuss
● Where's the most beautiful place on earth you've ever visited?
● What does this place say about Jesus, the Creator of all things?
● If Jesus is the 'image of the invisible God', what do you think God is like?

24 DEC

The servant king

Today's Advent reading picks up the theme of Jesus' simple and poor beginnings on earth and reminds us that humility and servanthood were the hallmarks of His ministry. These characteristics should also be a part of everyone who is a follower of Jesus.

The Word

All through His earthly ministry Jesus challenged the powerful. The Romans demanded total allegiance to the emperor. The wealthy, land-owning Sadducees demanded allegiance to the status quo. The pious Pharisees demanded allegiance to the observance of ritual. But Jesus wouldn't side with any of them. He refused to support their claims because His priority was the kingdom of heaven, not the kingdoms of the earth. His was a currency that dealt in sacrifice, humility and meekness and which threatened the established power structures, interest groups and political regimes of His day. Jesus said:

'You know that those who are regarded as the rulers of the Gentiles lord it over them, and their high officials exercise authority over them. Not so with you. Instead, whoever wants to become great among you must be your servant, and whoever wants to be first must be slave of all. For even the Son of Man did not come to be served, but to serve, and to give his life as a ransom for many' (Mark 10:42–45).

Read: Philippians 2:1–11.

Pause for thought

We live in a world in which many feel powerless and forgotten. The story of Jesus brings great strength and comfort to those who feel like this. He was not born in a palace but a stable. He didn't grow up among kings and princes but as a refugee in Egypt. He didn't walk the corridors of power but the road to the cross. He wasn't wealthy or of high social status; instead He mixed with tax collectors and prostitutes. This Jesus didn't just get alongside the powerless: He actually knew what it was to be marginalised by society.

Punch line

Jesus' own ministry was a demonstration of servanthood. The Lord of all creation came to earth in 'the very nature of a servant'. His life was lived in complete obedience to the will of His Father. This can speak poignantly to those who feel powerless, reassuring them that whatever their circumstances Jesus, the bringer of good news to the poor, is with them just where they are. We, His followers, are called to walk the same road: 'Your attitude should be the same as that of Christ Jesus' (Phil. 2:5).

A time to pray

Charles Wesley, the eighteenth-century evangelist, had an amazing ability to put the deepest and most complex aspects of Christian theology into verse. One of the most popular and famous Christmas carols, 'Hark the Herald Angels Sing', was written by him. We often sing it so heartily that we don't pause to reflect on the words. Today there is an opportunity to use two of the verses from his carol as a focus for your meditation …

Christ, by highest heaven adored,
Christ the everlasting Lord,
Late in time behold Him come,
Offspring of a Virgin's womb.
Veiled in flesh the Godhead see!
Hail, the incarnate Deity!
Pleased as man with men to dwell,
Jesus, our Emmanuel:

Hail, the heaven-born Prince of Peace!
Hail, the Sun of righteousness!
Light and life to all he brings,
Risen with healing in his wings.
Mild he lays his glory by,
Born that man no more may die,
Born to raise the sons of earth,
Born to give them second birth:

Pray for others
Pray for those who serve you in some way.

Reflect or discuss
● Describe incidents in the life of Jesus when He was a 'servant' to others.
● What did Jesus have to leave behind in order to 'empty himself' and 'make himself nothing'?
● What is it like to live 'the servant lifestyle'? Is servanthood the same as becoming a 'doormat' for others to 'walk all over'?

25 DEC

Christmas Day!

The Advent season reaches its consummation in the events of Christmas Day. The announcement that the Saviour, the Christ, has been born is good news to the world, but it demands a decision. Do you believe?

The Word
There has been a lot of debate about the 'virgin birth', but the reaction of Joseph lends considerable weight to our historic belief that Jesus was not conceived in the normal way. It is not the virgin birth that assures us that Jesus was great, it's the greatness of Jesus that points towards belief in the virgin birth!

There also has been much debate about the 'stable'. In the second century the Christian writer Justin Martyr stated that Jesus was born in a cave near the village of Bethlehem. Even now, in the area around Bethlehem, there are caves in the hills which are used as stables. Jesus was probably born in a 'cave stable' belonging to the innkeeper.[1]

Read: Luke 2:1–20.

Pause for thought
Many expected the Messiah to come with great splendour and glory. It was little wonder, then, that king Herod was so puzzled that Jesus

wasn't born in any of the places he'd have imagined! Jesus was born in obscurity because He had not come to replace king Herod as a political ruler. He had not come to fulfil the popular hope of a great military leader who might recapture Jerusalem and throw out the Romans!

No, Jesus was born among the poor, the hungry, the disadvantaged and the unloved. He came to an ordinary family among ordinary people. He came as a Saviour – on a rescue mission to redeem and to liberate.

Punch line

C.S. Lewis, one of England's greatest defenders of the faith, once wrote about Jesus:

A man who was merely a man and said the sort of things Jesus said would not be a great moral teacher. He would either be a lunatic – on a level with the man who says he is a poached egg – or else he would be the Devil of Hell. You must make your choice. Either this man was, and is, the Son of God: or else a madman or something worse. You can shut him up for a fool, you can spit at Him and kill Him as a Demon; or you can fall at His feet and call Him Lord and God. But let us not come with any patronising nonsense about His being a great human teacher. He has not left that open to us. He did not intend to.[2]

A time to pray

Today we use two Collects from the 1549 Prayer Book.

God, which makes us glad with the yearly remembrance of the birth of thy only Son Jesus Christ; grant that as we gratefully receive Him for our Redeemer, so we may with sure confidence behold Him, when He shall come to be our judge, who liveth and reigneth for ever.

Almighty God, which has given us Thy only begotten Son to take our nature upon Him, and this day to be born of a pure Virgin; Grant that we being regenerate, and made Thy children by adoption and grace, may daily be renewed by The Holy Spirit, through the same Lord Jesus Christ who liveth and reigneth for ever.

Pray for others

For those who are alone and lonely, homeless and without shelter, poor and without hope.

Christmas Day

> Pause to remember your own walk of faith. How did you come to know Jesus, to love Him and to follow Him? At your next Advent study group share faith-stories of how the 'Good News' came to you and how you've come to know Him as your Saviour.

26 DEC

The good shepherd!

It is poignant that some of the first people to be told of Christ's coming were shepherds. They were not the wealthy power brokers of the time; in fact they were often considered the lowest of the low. Jesus came to be our Shepherd. In our Advent journey today we recognise Him as our 'Good Shepherd'.

The Word

Shepherds held a special place in God's heart. For generations, the Jews had regarded God as the true Shepherd of the people of Israel. The writer of Psalm 23 compared Him to a 'good shepherd'. The prophets also saw the Messiah as someone who would have the same qualities of care and compassion as a good shepherd. Isaiah wrote:

See the Sovereign LORD comes with power, and his arm rules for him. See, his reward is with him, and his recompense accompanies him. He tends his flock like a shepherd: He gathers the lambs in his arms and carries them close to his heart; he gently leads those that have young (Isa. 40:10–11).

Read: Luke 2:17–20.

Pause for thought
Jesus fulfilled this great prophecy in Isaiah when He said, 'I am the good shepherd; I know my sheep and my sheep know me – just as the Father knows me and I know the Father – and I lay down my life for the sheep' (John 10:14–15).

Jesus is like a 'good shepherd' to us because He won't run away. The good shepherd fulfilled many important roles, but most importantly he always stayed with his flock. No matter what dangers were ahead, nor what wild animals approached, he stayed put. In Jesus' time a good shepherd always went before the flock. Unlike the shepherds in rural England who drive their sheep from the rear using whistles and sheep dogs, the Jewish shepherd led the way. The sheep trusted him so much that they followed the familiar call of his voice. Jesus goes ahead of us to show us the right way and to call us forward; He has that shepherd-like care for each of us.

Punch line
When sheep are troubled they look up to see if the shepherd is near. If they can't see him they become uneasy and are liable to panic. In Galilee today a shepherd will still fix a staff to the ground, place his coat around it and his headgear on the top to assure the sheep that he is near. The shepherd's presence means security and peace. Today, welcome Jesus into your life as your Shepherd, to stay with you, to guide you and to bring you security and peace.

A time to pray
Use the following words to reflect on the coming of the Shepherd King.

The King of love my Shepherd is,
Whose goodness faileth never;
I nothing lack if I am his
And he is mine forever.

Where streams of living water flow
My ransomed soul he leadeth,
And where the verdant pastures grow
With food celestial feedeth.

Perverse and foolish oft I strayed,
But yet in love he sought me,
And on his shoulder gently laid,
And home rejoicing brought me.

Henry Williams Baker (1821–77)

Pray for others
For those who feel lost and have no sense of direction.

Reflect or discuss
● What do you think it was like to be a shepherd at the time of Jesus?
● What effect do you think that the angelic vision had on the shepherds that night.
● In which ways can we know Jesus as our 'good shepherd'?

27 DEC

Come, Lord Jesus come!

Advent is the season to remember that Jesus not only came, but that He's coming again. He came the first time as a baby in a manger, but when He returns at the end of time He will come as our Lord and our Judge. So Advent should be a time of personal preparation in readiness for His return.

The Word
Three great Advent parables are all set at night. They involve a bridegroom, a returning master and a thief! All of them are solemn warnings that as followers of Jesus we should not take our ease but should be alert! They remind us that Advent is the season when we should review our lives, face up to our failures and prepare to meet Jesus face to face. A time to wake up and get ready!

Our reading today reminds us that life will continue to go on 'as normal' till Jesus returns. People will be getting married, men will be in the fields and women will be grinding corn. All blissfully unaware that history is about to end. We must be wide awake at all times – and ready to meet our Saviour!

Read: Luke 17:20–37

Pause for thought

We are preoccupied with mortality. We look in the mirror to trace the lines of our ageing. We sense the stiffness of the years, and our shortness of breath heralds the brevity of our existence. We are scared of the future, frightened about tomorrow. Our mortality stalks us, and creeps up on us just when we think we're safe.

The baby who stepped down from eternity rose up to take His place at God's right hand. While we are preoccupied with mortality, He occupies immortality. While we fear the future, He comes to greet us at the end of time – and to call us to account. He is the Lord of all eternity.

Punch line

Advent is a time for putting our hectic lives within the context of Christ's timelessness. For setting the insecurities of the future within the knowledge that He is already there waiting to greet us. For placing the passing chapters of human history within the story of His ultimate victory. All we can know is that He is coming soon, and our lives must be put in order in preparation for His return.

A time to pray

Our prayers today are a time of reflection based on two sections of the book of Revelation and a prayer. Relax and imagine!

Look, he is coming with the clouds, and every eye will see him, even those who pierced him; and all the peoples of the earth will mourn because of him. So shall it be! Amen.

'I am the Alpha and the Omega,' says the Lord God, 'who is, and who was, and who is to come, the Almighty' (Rev. 1:7–8).

'Behold, I am coming soon! My reward is with me, and I will give
to everyone according to what he has done. I am the Alpha and
the Omega, the First and the Last, the Beginning and the End'
(Rev. 22:12–13).

Lord, I'm preoccupied with time,
show me Your omniscience.
I'm preoccupied with fading things,
show me Your permanence.
I'm preoccupied with passing days,
show me Your immortality.
I'm preoccupied with future plans,
show me Your great design.
I'm preoccupied with my busyness,
show me Your eternity.

Pray for others
Pray that other Christians may come to recognise the shortness of the
time and the suddenness of Christ's return.

Reflect or discuss
● Do you think much about the future? Do you plan for the future?
  Do you look forward to it?
● What will the 'end of days' be like?
● If you knew you only had 24 hours to live, what would you do?

28 DEC

The intercessor

When He became incarnate as a human being Jesus was completely
immersed in human suffering. He left the riches of heaven for a
meagre stable and a homeless family. He was made flesh and in so
doing became frail and vulnerable. Because He shared our humanity,
He can really understand how we feel and can 'sympathise with our
weaknesses'. In our Advent journey today we discover a new
confidence to share everything with Him. By understanding

something of His priestly role we can gather strength for this important ministry.

The Word

The high priest at the time of Jesus could only enter the 'Holy of Holies' once a year, on the Day of Atonement. Even then, he had to have a rope tied around his waist in case he fainted so he could be pulled out. It was temporary access to the holy place where the ark of the covenant was – in a temple made by human hands.

Jesus is the Priest who entered *the* Holy Place – heaven itself. On the day of His crucifixion the curtain in the Holy of Holies was split into two, so that through Him we can all enter into God's holy presence! We can have confidence in our relationship with God because He is there, at the apex of all things. In the Holy of Holies. Not just for a day – but for eternity!

Read: Hebrews 4:14–5:10.

Pause for thought

Jesus is the High Priest who is at the right hand of God the Father. His prayers are made in the context of His intimate relationship as part of the Holy Trinity. He is the one mediator between us and God, He constantly makes intercession for His people.

'This is the confidence we have in approaching God: that if we ask anything according to his will, he hears us. And if we know that he hears us – whatever we ask – we know that we have what we asked of him' (1 John 5:14–15).

Punch line

Advent is a time for prayer, and a special season for intercession for others. It's good to know that Jesus still prays for us now. And when we pray, we join a prayer meeting that Jesus is already leading on our behalf!

Talkabout

If you are in a group, you could use the 'Reflect or discuss' sections from the last six days as a basis for discussion.

Meditation

On this 28th day of our Advent journey we pause to meditate rather
than to talk. You may like to light all four Advent candles and the
central Christmas candle at your meeting in a darkened room, play
some Christmas music on the stereo, and read our fourth Advent
meditation by candlelight!

Pause to think about what you have heard about the coming
of Jesus into the world and its significance for you over the last
seven days.

Prayer Link

From distant civilisations long gone to dust
You watch me now.
From future generations yet unborn
You come to me.

You stride across the centuries
And watch my earthly pilgrimage.
You see my life
From birth, to death
And in an instant see me come and go.

And so I look out
From this fleeting moment
And glimpse eternity.
And know again
That You,
My God,
Remember me.

Rob Frost

Coffee and chat

The most gruesome and sickening aspect of the Christmas story must
be the horrific incident which we know as the 'slaughter of the
innocents'. In a fit of uncontrolled anger Herod gave orders that all
the boys in Bethlehem and the surrounding area who were under
two years of age be killed. Matthew links this horrific incident to
Jeremiah's prophecy: '... Rachel weeping for her children and

refusing to be comforted, because they are no more' (Matt. 2:18).

This kind of violence against innocent children is an abhorrence. It stands in direct contradiction to the very basic standards of a civilised society. Yet, in the UK, since the abortion law was changed, over six million 'terminations' have been carried out. Abortion has seemingly become an everyday form of 'family planning'.

Evidence would suggest that, six weeks after fertilisation, the design for a human person is already visible. The cells are seething with life, the heart is beating, blood is being pumped through the umbilical cord and the whole embryo is in constant motion. The embryonic heart has 140–159 fluttering beats a minute – twice as many as its mother's.

By 18 weeks, though still a lightweight at 7 ounces, and only 6 inches long, the baby is now complete, needing only nourishment, warmth and a chance to grow. Infants as young as five months have survived premature births. Its mother begins to feel fluttering kicks and movements. And there is evidence that the baby hears outside noise.

What do you feel about abortion as a medical practice. What can we do if we disagree with it?

---

1. Justin Martyr (AD 100–165), *First Apology: Dialogue with Trypho.*

2. C.S. Lewis, *Mere Christianity* (New York: Macmillan Publishing Co., Inc. 1952), p.56.

Our Journey

29 DEC

Gifts for a king!

Jesus came to earth as King, but not the kind of king that Herod feared. For Christ was no ordinary king, and His was no ordinary kingdom! Our Advent journey today encourages us to discover Him as our King!

The Word

The Magi understood that they had come to find a very different kind of king. Their gifts symbolised the reign of someone very special. They brought gold, a gift which symbolised kingship. It was highly prized as far back as Abraham's time and coined since the time of Ezra. The Jews were mainly dependent on supplies of gold from Arabia, so it's little wonder that the Magi brought gold from their homeland. Gold for Jesus, the powerful King.

They brought frankincense, a resinous gum which was bitter to taste. It burns with a steady flame for a long time, and derives its name from the pleasant fragrance that it disseminates. It was found in Arabia and the Jews had used it for centuries as an ingredient of incense in their sacrificial offerings. It was a symbol of deity. Frankincense for Jesus, the sacrificial King.

Their third gift was myrrh, an aromatic resin. It was used with other spices for the anointing of holy things such as the Tent of Meeting, the ark, the table, the lampstand and the altar. It was also used for embalming the dead, including the body of Jesus (John 19:39). Myrrh for Jesus, the holy King.

Read: Matthew 2:1–12.

Pause for thought

These three precious gifts would have been inappropriate for a king like Herod, but they were just right for King Jesus. His kingdom isn't based on the power politics of petty regimes ... it is based on the eternal and lasting values of the kingdom of God!

Punch line

A humble girl called Mary knew what kind of king her son would become. She said, 'He will be great and will be called the Son of the Most High. The Lord God will give him the throne of his father David, and he will reign over the house of Jacob for ever; his kingdom will never end' (Luke 1:32–33).

This Christmas, welcome Jesus as your new-born King!

A time to pray

St Teresa of Avila was born in 1515. She was a great Christian mystic and many people today are blessed and encouraged by her writings. Once, she tried to describe her vision of the glorified Christ.

It is not a radiance which dazzles, but a soft whiteness and an infused radiance which, without wearying the eyes, causes them the greatest delight; nor are they wearied of the brightness which they see in seeing this Divine beauty ... It is a light which never gives place to light, and being always light, is disturbed by nothing.[1]

John, the author of Revelation, described his vision of King Jesus.

And when I turned I saw seven golden lampstands, and among the lampstands was someone 'like a son of man', dressed in a robe reaching down to his feet and with a golden sash round his chest. His head and hair were white like wool, as white as snow, and his eyes were like blazing fire. His feet were like bronze glowing in a furnace, and his voice was like the sound of rushing waters. In his right hand he held seven stars, and out of his mouth came a sharp double-edged sword. His face was like the sun shining in all its brilliance' (Rev. 1:12–16).

> **In your personal prayers worship Jesus Christ as King of kings!**

Lord, I can't imagine myself kneeling before a baby. I'm just too proud. Too intelligent. Too self-conscious. Too pre-occupied. Show me mercy. May I yet find time to kneel and worship Him, the King of kings, in sheer simplicity. Amen.

Pray for others

Every day Mother Theresa repeated a prayer that reminded her of the spiritual reality behind her acts of love. This prayer sums up what it means to make Jesus your King in everyday life.

Dearest Lord, may I see You today and every day in the person of Your sick, and while nursing them, minister unto You. Though You hide Yourself behind the unattractive guise of the irritable, the exacting, the unreasonable, may I still recognise You and say: 'Jesus, my patient, how sweet it is to serve You.'

Reflect or discuss

- If you have ever met 'royalty' or someone 'very important' what was it like?
- What do you think it would be like to meet 'King Jesus' face to face?
- What does it mean to recognise Jesus as your King in your everyday life?

30 DEC

Living the life!

As we near the end of our Advent journey, today's reading points us towards the kind of lives we should be living through this coming year.

The Word

The Jews in Colossae had been expounding a 'hollow and empty philosophy' based on religious practice, legalism and works. In his letter to them Paul reminds them that holiness does not come by such human effort, but through the power of Jesus Christ. Just as someone who joins the armed forces puts on a uniform, and so becomes easily recognisable, so all who follow Jesus Christ 'wear' a new lifestyle and a way of being which shows that we belong to Him.

Some of the aspects of this lifestyle include a new attitude towards other people – a life full of generosity and empathy. This life is expressed through love, peace, thanksgiving, worship and a loyalty to Christ which characterises who we are and how we live.

Read: Colossians 3:1–17.

Pause for thought

Those who are full of Christ are filled with a new security and peace. They long only to please God and to pour out their lives for others. This fullness enables them to rejoice in their suffering and tribulations and to prepare for Life Eternal.

John Habgood, in his book *Being a Person*, reminds us that everything about us – our identity, our continuity and our value are ultimately what they are because they are held in the mind of God.

Punch line

We can only live an 'Advent lifestyle' if we are willing to become empty of self and to open our lives so that we are full of Christ. Only then will we discover true fulfilment and wholeness and live the kind of life which brings glory to Him.

A time to pray

In your devotional time today, remember that there are things to leave behind:

sexual immorality
impurity
lust

evil desires
greed
anger
rage
malice
slander
filthy language
lying.

Pray for others
Think about how your life affects the lives of those around you. Pray for ways in which you might be a blessing to others. Pray for more compassion, kindness, humility, gentleness, patience, forbearance, forgiveness, and love ...

Reflect or discuss
● Have you ever met anyone who seemed to live a genuinely 'Christian lifestyle'? What impressed you most about them?
● Which three of these do you think you need most? Compassion, kindness, humility, gentleness, patience, forbearance, forgiveness, and love ...
  Why?
● Share your lists together – and pray!

31 DEC

Where there is no vision!

As we end our Advent journey our minds turn towards the new year and the new opportunities which await us! Today, in preparation for the year that lies ahead, we focus on the prayer of Jabez.

The Word
Jabez was a real person. He was a man of faith and a man of prayer. He and his mother lived a pain-stricken life, in a turbulent and difficult era. His story is of one man's relentless pursuit to serve God throughout his life.

Read: 1 Chronicles 4:9–10

The core of his famous prayer says, 'Oh, that you would bless me and enlarge my territory!' In his profound little book, *The Prayer of Jabez*, Bruce Wilkinson sums up this plea very simply:

The Jabez prayer is a revolutionary request. Just as it is highly unusual to hear anyone pray, 'God, please bless me!' so it is rare to hear anyone plead, 'God, please give me more ministry!' Most of us think our lives are too full already. But when, in faith, you start to pray for more ministry, amazing things occur. As your opportunities expand, your ability and resources supernaturally increase, too.[2]

Pause for thought

This kind of vision for our lives and our service for God doesn't come as a programme which is dropped from the sky in a conveniently wrapped ready-to-use package. It's something which God grows in us and builds from our previous life experience.

George Barna once wrote in *The Power of Vision*: 'Vision for ministry is a clear mental image of a preferable future imparted by God to His chosen servants and is based upon an accurate understanding of God, self, and circumstances.'

Why not ask God to 'broaden your territory' over the coming year, and why don't you seek an even greater vision for your own life and ministry. Too many of us have set our borders too close to our own backyard. We live in our own pre-selected comfort zone, and shiver at the thought of God wanting to do anything greater through us next year than He did last year.

Punch line

Ultimately, vision is not enough. Vision must become action or it is completely useless. A Christian leader once said:

Vision without action is merely a dream.
Action without vision just passes the time.
Vision with action can change the world!

Over the coming year think big! We've got a big God!

A time to pray

> Commit the following year to the Lord, and ask Him to give you a
> bigger vision for serving Him!

In his hymnbook dated 20 October 1797, John Wesley had written
that he hoped the compilation of hymns within would be 'a means
of raising or quickening the spirit of devotion; of confirming his
faith; of enlivening his hope; and of kindling or enlivening his love
to God and man'. Our journey through Advent ends with one of
those hymns. It is his brother Charles Wesley's great hymn for a new
year and it is in itself a wonderful prayer for the coming year.

Come, let us anew
Our journey pursue,
Roll round with the year,
And never stand still till the Master appears.

His adorable will
Let us gladly fulfil,
And our talents improve,
By the patience of hope and the labour of love.

Our life is a dream,
Our time as a stream
Glides swiftly away,
And the fugitive moment refuses to stay.

The arrow is flown,
The moment is gone;
The millennial year
Rushes on to our view, and eternity's here.

O that each in the day
Of his coming may say:

'I have fought my way through,
I have finished the work thou didst give me to do!'

O that each from his Lord
May receive the glad word:
'Well and faithfully done;
Enter into my joy, and sit down on my throne'!

Ask God to give you new opportunities for ministry in the coming year.

Pray for others
● For those in your close family.
● In your Advent study group.

Reflect or discuss
● What plans, if any, have you got for the coming year?
● How can each of us 'move forward' in our walk with God?
● Do you agree with the idea that if you pray for 'more ministry' God will give you grace to meet the new challenge?

---

1. Quoted in *Stairway to Heaven*, Mary Batchelor (Hodder & Stoughton, 1999) p.214.

2. Bruce Wilkinson, *The Prayer of Jabez* (Multnomah Press, 2000).

National Distributors

UK: (and countries not listed below)
CWR, Waverley Abbey House, Waverley Lane, Farnham, Surrey GU9 8EP.
Tel: (01252) 784700 Outside UK (44) 1252 784700

AUSTRALIA: CMC Australasia, PO Box 519, Belmont, Victoria 3216. Tel: (03) 5241 3288

CANADA: Cook Communications Ministries, PO Box 98, 55 Woodslee Avenue, Paris, Ontario. Tel: 1800 263 2664

GHANA: Challenge Enterprises of Ghana, PO Box 5723, Accra. Tel: (021) 222437/223249 Fax: (021) 226227

HONG KONG: Cross Communications Ltd, 1/F, 562A Nathan Road, Kowloon. Tel: 2780 1188 Fax: 2770 6229

INDIA: Crystal Communications, 10-3-18/4/1, East Marredpalli, Secunderabad – 500026, Andhra Pradesh.
Tel/Fax: (040) 27737145

KENYA: Keswick Books and Gifts Ltd, PO Box 10242, Nairobi. Tel: (02) 331692/226047 Fax: (02) 728557

MALAYSIA: Salvation Book Centre (M) Sdn Bhd, 23 Jalan SS 2/64, 47300 Petaling Jaya, Selangor.
Tel: (03) 78766411/78766797 Fax: (03) 78757066/78756360

NEW ZEALAND: CMC Australasia, PO Box 36015, Lower Hutt. Tel: 0800 449 408 Fax: 0800 449 049

NIGERIA: FBFM, Helen Baugh House, 96 St Finbarr's College Road, Akoka, Lagos.
Tel: (01) 7747429/4700218/825775/827264

PHILIPPINES: OMF Literature Inc, 776 Boni Avenue, Mandaluyong City. Tel: (02) 531 2183 Fax: (02) 531 1960

REPUBLIC OF IRELAND: Scripture Union, 40 Talbot Street, Dublin 1. Tel: (01) 8363764

SINGAPORE: Armour Publishing Pte Ltd, Block 203A Henderson Road, 11–06 Henderson Industrial Park,
Singapore 159546. Tel: 6 276 9976 Fax: 6 276 7564

SOUTH AFRICA: Struik Christian Books, 80 MacKenzie Street, PO Box 1144, Cape Town 8000.
Tel: (021) 462 4360 Fax: (021) 461 3612

SRI LANKA: Christombu Books, 27 Hospital Street, Colombo 1. Tel: (01) 433142/328909

TANZANIA: CLC Christian Book Centre, PO Box 1384, Mkwepu Street, Dar es Salaam. Tel/Fax (022) 2119439

ZIMBABWE: Word of Life Books, Shop 4, Memorial Building, 35 S Machel Avenue, Harare.
Tel: (04) 781305 Fax: (04) 774739

For email addresses, visit the CWR website: www.cwr.org.uk

CWR is a registered charity – number 294387

Trusted
All Over the World

Daily Devotionals

Books and Videos

Day and Residential Courses

Counselling Training

Biblical Study Courses

Regional Seminars

Ministry to Women

CWR have been providing training and resources for Christians since the 1960s. From our headquarters at Waverley Abbey House we have been serving God's people with a vision to help apply God's Word to everyday life and relationships. The daily devotional *Every Day with Jesus* is read by over three-quarters of a million people in more than 150 countries, and our unique courses in biblical studies and pastoral care are respected all over the world.

For a free brochure about our seminars and courses or a catalogue of CWR resources please contact us at the following address.

CWR,
Waverley Abbey House,
Waverley Lane,
Farnham,
Surrey GU9 8EP, UK

Telephone: +44 (0)1252 784700
Email: mail@cwr.org.uk
Website: www.cwr.org.uk

Here and Now
Rob Frost

One of the most inspiring books on the Beatitudes
you will ever read. Rob Frost's fresh approach to the
opening to Christ's Sermon on the Mount relates
these timeless truths to our experiences in the
twenty-first century. *Here & Now* will challenge you
emotionally, delight you intellectually and strengthen
you spiritually.

£3.99 (plus p&p)
ISBN: 1-85345-236-X

EDWJ for New Christians
Selwyn Hughes

A powerful and relevant guide for people new to the Christian faith or for people who need the basics presented to them clearly and dynamically. A favourite with churches across denominations.

£1.99 (plus p&p)

ISBN: 1-85345-133-9

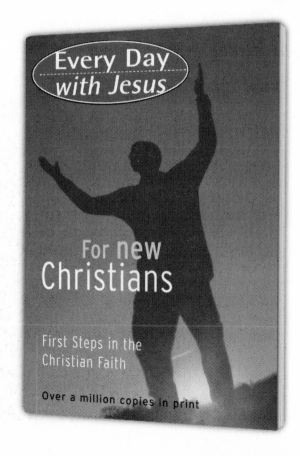

EDWJ for People in Search of God
Selwyn Hughes

This is a great tool for friendship evangelism, because when it comes to those hard, demanding questions people want clear, thoughtful answers. This guide offers an intelligent and helpful perspective on those big issues,

- What is life all about?
- Is there life after death?
- Who is God and what is He like?
- How can we know God?
- Why does God allow suffering?

£1.99 (plus p&p)

ISBN: 1-85345-226-2

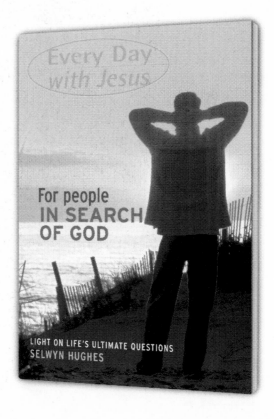